MEET ME AT
THE BUTTERFLY TREE

A fairhope Memoir

MEET ME AT
THE BUTTERFLY TREE

A Fairhope Memoir

Mary Lois Timbes

and

Robert E. Bell

Over the Transom
2001

Over the Transom Publishing Company
323 De La Mare Avenue
Fairhope, AL 36532
email: letters@overthetransom.com

Meet Me at the Butterfly Tree: A Fairhope Memoir
Copyright © 2001 by Mary Lois Timbes

Library of Congress Control Number: 2001097707
ISBN 0-9643727-8-9

Manufactured in the United States of America

Typeset in Goudy Old Style
Design and composition by
Suzanne S. Barnhill, Words into Type
Cover design by MaryLou Hyland

First Edition 2001

10 9 8 7 6 5 4 3 2 1

All too soon
The village becomes the town,
And our cherished local color, individuality, and quaintnesses
Blend and tone down
Until little remains to distinguish us from our neighbors.

Mary Heath Lee, Fairhope, 1928

Acknowledgments

UCH TIME IN THE PREPARATION OF THIS BOOK was spent in talking with many people about Fairhope and the many specific people mentioned herein. I am indebted to Nancy Calhoun Cain for putting me in touch with some of those who shared their stories of Fairhope that I would use in the book and for her constant urging that I get to work and get the book finished.

I thank Helene Beiser Hunter, Evalyn Berglin Turner, Joyce Totten Bishop, Claire Totten Gray, Camilla Bishop, and Sally Patterson Lieberman. I am grateful to Flo Simmons and the archives at the Fairhope History Museum, and to Annie Lowrie Sheldon, Dean Mosher, Pagan Sheldon Mosher, and Aline Riggs. Many memories were recalled with the help of my sister, Billye, and my brother, Graham.

The material at the Marietta Johnson Museum was extremely helpful, as were the recollections of Dorothy Beiser ("Mama Dot") Cain and others who participate in keeping the history of the Organic School. Paul Gaston's book *Women of Fair Hope* was a wonderful and useful reference. Janet McGrath's unpublished thesis, "A School for Utopia," at the Marietta Johnson Museum, was helpful in providing information and jogging my own memory. Special thanks is due to

Cathy Donelson, who read the original manuscript and helped me reorganize and edit the book.

In acknowledging those who helped make a book possible, the danger of omission looms. The people who really made it possible to write this were those who were there in Fairhope, both before I came and during the experiences I describe here, those I observed in the halcyon days that became "old Fairhope" while nobody was looking.

Mary Lois Timbes

2001

Foreword

PICTURESQUE LITTLE FAIRHOPE attracts by a certain atmosphere—a comfort, a beauty, a spirit—that exists *in the air*.
There is something different about it. Just under the surface,
beneath the freshly planted flowers and newly placed flags, lies
something intriguing that we can't quite define but that seems almost
universally experienced.

Shadows remain of an odd collection of people, characters too
strange to be fictitious, the citizens of Old Fairhope. A hermit who
lived five miles to the north walked into town barefooted to attend
lectures and forums. A lady lived in a tree house in the center of
town. A veterinarian who was also trained as an opera singer made
house calls on her white horse, occasionally stopping to converse in
French with other Francophones in the village. There was a piano
teacher who had appeared on the New York stage, and a scientist who
was once a dancer in Isadora Duncan's troupe. A lanky professor who
rolled his own cigarettes held teenagers spellbound on everything from
Civil War history to the Stanislavski Method. A housewife who often
dressed in flamboyant gypsy garb claimed to be a medium, conjuring
up people from the Other Side who told her where gold was buried.
These people lived in Fairhope, and the remarkable thing is that they

were hardly considered remarkable. They were accepted as ordinary citizens.

You can feel their impact today. Their ideas set them apart. Their original thinking brought them together to form the community. These people and others of their ilk left traces that tell of all that Fairhope once was.

Fairhope's early years must have been extraordinary. Fairhope attracted those with experimental dreams, a penchant for the unusual. Many early settlers were mavericks, gadflies, old-time radicals with a "purpose grand to redeem the land," as the old song, "Fairhope," says.

Descriptions of the village that was Fairhope in the early twentieth century fairly palpitate with a love of the place itself, its pines, its gullies and cliffs—and the Bay lapping against the beach soothingly, granting assurance that life is good and peace is possible. And it is this same reverence for the area binds us to those pioneers today.

In this era of rapid change, let us hope that the town does not lose its memory altogether. Without preserving the ideas that brought it into being, without attention to critical thought and even eccentricity, without some cantankerous complaints from the locals, Fairhope just wouldn't be Fairhope. Perhaps a look at the past can show us what Fairhope can become.

It is difficult to remember that at one time Fairhope attracted visitors not just because it was pleasant in the winter but because it was cooler than other places in the summer. Before air conditioning was common, the people treasured Bay breezes, went outside their houses, and sat on porches, feeling the moist air as a pleasure and the closeness to the Mobile Bay a visual and sensual treat. Children and adults frolicked off the Big Wharf and into the Bay, splashing its warm waters; wading, swimming, and squealing with abandon.

The town was threaded with gullies that offered unlimited opportunities for children—hidden places to pretend, to climb, to swing on vines, to explore, stretch, and grow. Even the grownups took walks through the gullies, and showed them off to visitors from other places that were not fortunate enough to have gullies of their own.

Robert E. Bell's novel *The Butterfly Tree* was set in a Fairhope that I hope is not gone forever. Its title alludes to a place where a magical butterfly tree grows. When one finds the tree, the secrets of life's beauty and meaning are captured for a moment for all that find it through an individual quest. Bob Bell lived and died believing this place was Fairhope, and that he had found his own answers here.

I have seen many butterflies come and go in Fairhope, leaving and returning. I too have lived around the world only to return in order to seek the best life I can live. Like all good myths, the butterfly tree symbol has some basis in truth.

By providing information that will intrigue and inform about the Fairhope of old, I hope to inspire an intellectual rebirth. Even better, perhaps these people we remember will have a renewal of influence and help us recapture our feeling of the village Fairhope once was.

Mary Lois Timbes
Fairhope, Alabama 2001

The Letters

November 12, 1993

Dear Mr. [Robert E.] Bell,

I'm writing in connection with a project celebrating Fairhope's Centennial year, 1994. Butch Sheldon has already contacted you about this and passed your letter of recollections on to me. Perhaps she sent you a copy of the enclosed proposal outlining our plans.

Thank you so much for the time and patience you've already shown in your thoughtful letter. I hope you'll continue to work with us as we move forward.

I grew up in Fairhope in the 1950s and returned in 1988. I'd like to see the Centennial used as a way to inform all these newcomers of the true heritage of Fairhope, its commitment to nonconformity and a life of the mind—whether or not anyone is ever able to recapture it.

Anyway, I'm writing the segment of our presentation that deals with Gretchen Riggs, so if you have any anecdotes, biographical info, or other Gretchenisms that you recall, please make note of them for me. Her daughter lives here now* and she let me see a scrapbook of poetry Gretchen wrote in the early 1920s—passionate, Edna St. Vinc ent

---

*Gail Riggs Remaley died in 1998.

1

Millay–type stuff that astonished me. We'd also love to have Winifred's poems, excerpts from her letters, whatever.

For your information, I bought a hardcover copy of *The Butterfly Tree* when it was first published. I recall you as a friend of Virginia Austin, who was the mother of one of my classmates. Virginia died a year or so ago. I did contact Andrew Dacovich, too, who lives in Mobile now. He was very sweet, but I got the impression he doesn't remember much—or that maybe he didn't want to reveal too much.† Did you know Clayton Corzatte? I have no doubt he influenced me to be involved in theatre (as did Gretchen Riggs and the wonderful Fairhope Little Theatre of those days, with performances in Comings Hall. How I miss that place whenever we gather for events in the cold Municipal Center, built as a supermarket by Delchamps in the 1960s.)

Well, I'm falling all over myself trying to impress you. I know that sometimes has the opposite effect, but let the proposal do the impressing. Just say you'll help us as we proceed with this project. The plan is to produce the event in March, so this is the time for digging and writing drafts, etc. I'll be happy to keep you up to date on who's still around in Fairhope and what they're doing.

Cordially,
Mary Lois Adshead

1 December 93

Dear Mary Lois:

And don't I love Southern names that call for a first name and a middle name—like Billy Joe, Betty Sue, and Mary Lois...You didn't need to go to any trouble to "impress" me. I am, of course, pleased that you have a hardback copy of *The Butterfly Tree*. If you still have the dust jacket intact, these are going for about $35 these days. I have

---

†Andrew Dacovich, a Mobile chiropractor and supporter of the arts, died in 1999.

five original Andy Warhol drawings for the cover, and I have no idea what they are worth...

I like you already for your interest in recovering the old Fairhope I knew when I was growing up. We lived in Birmingham, and every summer, even during the Depression, we came down and stayed at places like the old Casino (50 cents per night) or the Kanuck Hotel (on Fairhope Avenue just below Moyer's Drugstore) or, finally, Nicholsville Lodge, the charming cottages along the bayfront run by Georgia Nichols and her daughters Alice and Madelyn. Fairhope was such a magic place to us that we finally moved there in 1947, to Summit Street between Kiefer and Powell. We paid $3,000 for the house, which I understand recently sold for $78,000.

I was there during the great days, depending on whose great days you are talking about. Mary Heath Lee was still the librarian of the Fairhope Public Library, assisted by Ruth Jeffcott. The Casino was still there. The end of the big pier was still a mass of burned-out pilings. A boat still took people on a nightly cruise from the middle of the pier. There was still a movie house. You still had to pick up your mail at the post office, since there was no door-to-door delivery. There was the Pinequat Shop, run by an old lady and her daughter, and we were never sure which was the mother and which was the daughter. The Soda Garden was the hangout spot for everyone. The Parker House was where you went after all events.

Gretchen Riggs was a kind of guru. I kept hearing about her, but somehow we didn't meet until years later. Winifred knew her and learned that she was doing puppets. We went to call on her. She was subject to enthusiasms, and suddenly it was puppets. I worked at the Mobile Library, and checked out everything I could find for her. She wanted to model puppets from scratch, and this is where Winifred could help, since Winifred was into sculpture. The formula called for sawdust and some kind of adhesive and formaldehyde. We dutifully modeled puppets at her house once a week. Ruth Jeffcott was also there. We ended up with an ensemble suitable for putting on a little show. We invited Converse and Edith Harwell, maybe the Sheldons, and one or two other people. The show was, "Soldier, Soldier, Will You Marry Me," and I still flinch from my miserable singing voice.

Ruth was the maiden. The whole thing took less than five minutes, but it was a triumph for Gretchen.

I kept in touch with her after I left Fairhope. I think we corresponded when I was in Fort Worth. But Gretchen was never really in my life, as were Winifred and Anna. We vastly respected each other, but we were never intimate. My puppet experience with her was about the extent of the relationship.

Fairhope was a dream world that came true for me. I don't think just everyone can say that.

Sincerely,
Bob Bell

May 9, 1994‡

Dear Mary Lois:

Please forgive me for answering immediately, since many people (not you) who don't write letters often consider instant answers a kind of imperative to do the same. It's just that some of the things you said stirred a response that might be lost in a letter at a later time...

We moved to Fairhope from Birmingham in 1947 when I was twenty, so I really can't qualify as a bona fide old Fairhopian. But in another way I can, since we had come to Fairhope since I was a baby (sand in my diapers) during summers and even a couple of winters. Fairhope was my dream place from my earliest memories. I looked at it as a kind of nirvana and never believed that we would actually move there. When we did, I thought I had bypassed all the slings and arrows and gone straight to heaven. We lived at 252 N. Summit in a little house that cost us $3,500. (It recently sold for around $89,000!)§ The street

---

‡The author, wanting readers to focus on what Bob Bell had to say, has omitted a number of her own letters. The content, like that of the other side of a half heard phone conversation, can be inferred from Bell's responses. *Editor*

§In 2001, similar properties in the neighborhood are being offered at $500,000 or more.

was unpaved, we had no telephone, and we heated with a fireplace and oil heaters. It was entirely glorious. I think the population was around 2,500. We had to walk uptown to the post office. We had a car, but I hadn't learned to drive. My brothers and I went to the old movie house. We walked down the wooden steps leading from Bayview and Powell—or was it Kiefer?—and spent lots of time at the Little Wharf (in the park) and the Big Pier. We *lived* in the Soda Garden. It was purely idyllic.

I had to return to Birmingham to finish Birmingham-Southern, but I LIVED to come home on weekends and vacations, either thumbing or taking the Hummingbird. Even Mobile was still a rather small place (pop. 78,000). Bienville Square was an oasis, not a place to worry about your safety. You could sit there, maybe even eat lunch from a brown bag, and watch the world go past. After I had been there a while I could visit the studios of William Bush, Genevieve Southerland, and Ed DeCelle just up the street on Dauphin. Julian Lee Rayford still had a studio over the Haunted Bookshop on Conception. Cammie Plummer was a little girl who had a stall outside the Haunted Bookshop called Cammie's Rive Gauche Bookstall.

Back to Fairhope. I got to know Anna Braune, Barbara Key (whom everyone seems to have forgotten), and King Benton. King was a major turning point in my life. She didn't live in Fairhope but in Daphne. But her kids, Diana and Daniel, went to Fairhope High School. She acted in *Rebecca* for the Fairhope Little Theatre and later directed *You Can't Take It With You*, which was one of the high points in the theatre's history. Somebody should certainly do a history of her, and I suppose I should be the one since I knew her best. Incidentally, her ambition was to do *A Midsummer Night's Dream* in the little amphitheatre on the Daphne beach….

The last time I came to Fairhope I was not happy with what I saw on the main street, but then I drove around the old neighborhoods and saw how little they had changed. The years dropped away, and suddenly I was back in the old days. I suspect there is still a lot of hope…

Well, I am running on and on. Briefly, I share your concern. But, good lord, where were you in those old Soda Garden days? We must have rubbed shoulders a thousand times. Were you the pretty girl in the next booth?

Sincerely,
Bob

May 27, 1994

Dear Mary Lois:

Yes, I was 20 when we moved to Fairhope in 1947, so I certainly do have a few years on you. I remember Kenny Cain but not very well. I loved the Soda Garden and was sorry to see it go. I also loved the old Central Café, the old post office, the Pinequat Shop, and many other places that seemed to disappear one by one.

I came home from Harvard in 1951 and worked at the Mobile Public Library until 1955, when I moved to Fort Worth. From there I went to San Francisco and then back to the Gulf Coast in 1962. I bought the house on the northwest corner of Pier and Pomelo. I lived there a couple of years while I worked again at the Mobile Public. Then I moved to New Orleans, attended LSU for a second master's, and then returned to San Francisco to enter the doctoral program at UC Berkeley. You can see I have had a rather nomadic existence.

It is interesting that you should mention Clayton Corzatte. I never knew him in Fairhope, but my brother Billy ran around with a crowd that included his sister Bobbie. Clayton later made a name for himself, and his springboard role was the juvenile lead (Tony) in *You Can't Take It With You*. I thought it was Barter Theatre, but I guess not. I played that same role in the Fairhope Little Theatre. This was a grand experience. King Benton directed. Anna Braune was the Russian countess. Craig Sheldon was in it. Temple Graham, Grandpa Thomas, Ray Gartman, Marge Nahrgang, Lillian Dent, Kitty Coulon, Andrew Dacovich, Dan Benton, and others. I finally did meet Clayton, but it was in Seattle a few years ago. One of my best friends was fund-raising, principally for the Seattle Repertory Theatre, and once when I visited him they were doing *The Front Page*, in which Clayton had a

6

large role. I spoke to him briefly backstage afterwards. It is interesting that King's daughter, Diane, lived in Seattle at that time; I visited her that same trip.

It's too bad you missed King. She was one of the great turning points in my life. I guess I was really in love with her, although she was a couple of years older than my mother and although I was briefly engaged to Diane. King had worked in the theatre for most of her adult life—all the way from melodramas to legitimate theatre and even circuses. She could hold you spellbound for hours. Her husband Dan was a violinist with the Mobile symphony, but he still performed with her some of their old show biz numbers, and it was a delight to be there when they got turned on. They were both alcoholics, so that was rather often…

I remember Burkel's *before* it was a roller rink. It even had slot machines back when.

Well, I'll hush for now…

Take care,
Bob

July 3, 1994

Dear Mary Lois:

Your letter was great…I'm sure our paths crossed many a time, but the age difference certainly meant mainly separate paths…

I love your account of your Monroeville trip. I know Harper Lee. She and I have communicated ever since 1959, and I met her (and Truman Capote) once on the town square in Monroeville. It was back when the earth was cooling. They were on their way somewhere, and we didn't have too much of a chance to talk. I think it is great to have the *Mockingbird* courthouse scene reenacted, and I think it would be great to have Truman's short stories read, especially "Children on Their Birthdays," my personal favorite. When I last talked to Nelle, she seemed somehow distanced from Truman. Knowing her, I suspect that his excesses were a little much, and she probably joined everyone else in thinking he should have kept *Answered Prayers* to himself. She is really quite conservative—even a Republican. Of course I love her, since in her last letter to me she said that she thought *The Butterfly Tree* was a "glimpse of perfection." I mean, coming from a Pulitzer Prize winner, that is the greatest compliment I could imagine. As for the writing of *To Kill a Mockingbird*, I would love to take credit. I know there has been speculation about Truman Capote's role, but I think it was merely advisory. I think she wrote every word, but maybe he had a say in what she edited out or included. He was a consummate craftsman. I had a good friend who helped me in this way on my novel. Even though she couldn't herself write, she had great perceptions and exquisite taste. Writers often get carried away and are lacking in judgment.

I wish I could have been there for *Midsummer Night's Dream*. Probably only in Fairhope could such magic happen. Try to think of this play anywhere else in an outdoor setting—without the loom of cypresses, the fragrance of jessamine, the face of the moon, the susurrus of waves lapping on the shore. I commend you for making this happen...

The other thing: the kids of Fairhope. My first experience was just after I moved there. Barbara Key, a long-forgotten teacher at Fairhope High (then in the middle of downtown) conceived of a summer thing for her students and ex-students. This was a farce called *Out of the Frying Pan*. I got conscripted because I was young and handsome and recently out of high school and didn't know how to say no, and I played a dumb cop. This way I met everyone in Fairhope. And the kids were marvelous. I mean freshmen from Auburn and Alabama, not to mention the ones still in Fairhope High, like Dickie Dryer. You know, I doubt if anyone has ever done a study of theatre as a socializing force. In the winter I got another role, Jack Favelle in *Rebecca* and then Tony in *You Can't Take It With You*. I guess I owe it to the theatre for my Fairhope integration, for I met the Sheldons, the Harwells, the Nicholses, the Gastons, King Benton, Anna Braune, and eventually Gretchen Riggs...

I have gone on too long. I tend to do this with special people. Maybe we should think of *The Butterfly Tree* for a beach thing. Maybe we should not. Someone remarked once that it should be a ballet. Who knows? With a talent for the impossible—like yours—it is an altogether possibility.

Lovingly,
Bob

July 11, 1994

Dear Bob,

I'm sure you know I enjoy getting your letters at least as much as you enjoy getting mine. It's such fun to compare notes—there is excitement and joy in what you write and in my reading of it; then the fun of responding. I simply have to hold myself back sometimes. Maybe I'm a letter addict.

There was such a pause before I received your last that I amused myself by re-reading *The Butterfly Tree*! There's an advantage you have over most correspondents. It was like a letter from the past, describing places in Fairhope, some of which I hadn't thought about in ages. For instance, young Peter gets off the bus at the Fairhope bus station. I knew exactly where that was, and, in fact, the little building is empty and has been for years. It's one of those spots one looks at and wants to buy, for some reason. A little piece of what is now "old" Fairhope. I just caught myself sighing as I wrote that…

Do you have a play in your trunk? Reading *The Butterfly Tree* I thought, as you seem to have, "Maybe we could stage some of this…," but so much is out on the beach, in the creeks and gullies, etc., and it's not theatrical, as so much is in the narration. It could be a *Glass Menagerie*–type thing—but that's been done before. Maybe my favorite character is Eulacie. Obviously TBT (new abbreviation for it?) would be lovely as a movie, but I think it best to move on to other things…

I know there's a great deal we don't know about each other—that's one reason it's so exciting to have such a rapport. Early on I wrote

9

that I was in school with Vicki Austin, daughter of Virginia, and you were the exciting young novelist who was hanging out with the old ladies that year (and other years I guess). When TBT was actually published there was such excitement! I think Virginia was miffed that she wasn't in it. Or was she? Maybe she was Mr. Bloodgood.

I love your immediate and irrefutable response to me. It's people like you who make people like me possible. Then we go and do the impossible, and it was you who made it possible...This is beginning to sound like I'm drinking. I'd better quit before anybody notices.

Love,
Mary Lois

July 28, 1994

Dear Mary Lois:

...I am pleased that you reread *The Butterfly Tree* and that invoked so many happy memories. I, too, look at the old bus station on Section and would love to buy it. Maybe I will if it's still standing when and if I return to Fairhope for the final countdown. And that is a possibility. I think I just might turn it into a studio and sit and write and ponder...That is where I met King Benton the first night we rehearsed *Rebecca* (Andrew Dacovich, director). My father used to work in Melton's Garage next door. I used to leave from there each morning for work across the Bay...

Vicki Austin. Well, I do remember her and Timmy. It so happened I was in Mobile when I read in the paper about Timmy's death. I had to remember Virginia's flat-out statement that he was a genius. I knew Timmy and am afraid I never saw him in that light. I used to ride the bus to Mobile with Crider, who kept saying I should meet his wife, and that's how I got to know Virginia. I was in the bar next to the Creamery one night and Crider suddenly appeared with Virginia, who looked deep into my eyes and said without ceremony, "You have seen the Brahmic Light." I wasn't sure that I had but felt nervous about admitting that. They later moved down on the bayfront and I spent many an evening waiting for the séance table to tap out messages. You do know that she got a message finally and dug up half of old Blakeley looking for buried treasure. God, has anyone ever done Fairhope justice?

As for sounding like you're drinking. Don't worry about it, even if you should be. I have a drinking problem—why not, with two grandfathers who dropped dead from the effects, and assorted uncles. I went to AA but had a problem with the self-righteous tone of reformed alcoholics. I still drink an occasional glass of wine (if it's free) but it is no longer important. My compulsion to work at writing overrides everything else.

I vastly enjoyed your last letter. I don't think I need to tell you I look forward to the next one.

Love,
Bob

16 August 94

Dear Mary Lois:

We are joined at the navel, I am sure. Virtually every paragraph in your letter summoned up *recherche de temps perdu*. Since you admit you are not a reader, that is a reference to Proust, who, by the way, *nobody* ever reads even though they talk about him ad nauseam. I am trying to read him, but he has to be the world's dullest writer—all 2000 pages of him; I will never make it in this lifetime.

I am sorry the old bus station has been turned into a nifty-gifty, but I can understand why someone would seize the opportunity. I, too, wish they had called it Bus Stop Antiques or something like that. "They," of course, stalk our dreams and try to find anything they can to destroy...

Hey, don't worry. You didn't say anything much about drinking in your letter. But I picked up on your clue, when you mentioned drinking: "there's another story." I figured there was. I want to amend my statement about AA. I think it is probably one of the greatest concepts ever developed. When I first "enrolled" I was crazy about it. It in itself almost became addictive. I went to meetings and was often the chair. It was only later that I began to wonder if I needed to listen to all the recitals of failed marriages and failed lives...I stayed with it for three years at least but left because of all the AA egos...I still support the idea of AA and still practice its principles, even though at this moment I am sipping a glass of white wine.

Your house on Bayview. I think it was the opposite end of the gully that gnawed its way up on Bayview. There was a huge tree right there. In my book, the fireflies drifted out of the gully like the souls of dead sailors or something like that. It was in that very spot, even though I might not have had your house in mind. Whatever, that short stretch of bayfront will remain as one of the magic places of all time in my memory. Incidentally, the house we had at 254 N. Summit...is on the market currently for over $100,000. I would have held onto it forever, but my mother had to move out when she overheard the woman next door being killed by her husband. He broke a beer bottle over her head, and Mother heard the fatal blow. After that nothing would do except they had to sell the house and move...Kanuck was a "hotel." That's where we stayed sometimes when we came down from Birmingham. Once the whole family and later my father and I. It had airless little rooms on a second floor, and we slept there. We loved it because it was a quick walk down to the Bay and also handy to "uptown."...Julwin's. Yes, it was Dale's. I used to drink late there. And that was, as I said, where I met Virginia Austin. At that time they lived in a little house on Fairhope Avenue next to Pope's Grocery. Later they moved to one of those spooky old bayfront houses near Burkel's, and we used to do séances there.

It seems that plans for getting together with my brothers have been shoved into later fall, so I guess I won't be seeing you perform. But maybe another time. I *will* be seeing you, however, when I do come...

Love,
Bob

August 24, 1994

Dear Bob,

You won't believe this, but even **Proust** is a shared hang-up, or at least a shared reference—and exactly in the context of your last letter.

...Let me use the next page to address Fairhope questions and situations. I really don't think my house was the TBT house, but I'll bet it's one of the nearby neighbors. Lots of tearing down and rebuilding along that street, unfortunately. The older homes, many of them, are owned by single elderly women; when they go the nouveaus will have their way and remake the street.

I was going to write an article for some publication—too bad an appropriate one doesn't exist—describing the secret war between the two factions in Fairhope. I call them the Nouveaus and the Fairhos. People I describe it to are tickled at the appellations, but I haven't really developed my theme further. Wanted to do a quiz defining the two: "Have you ever described Fairhope as 'a charming little Disneyland town'?" (Nouveau), or "Would you welcome an eccentric intellectual to speak to your study group?" (Fairho)

...I guess you know the Colonial Inn was demolished. If you didn't know, that's a crushing blow, as it was to the community...The Centennial celebrations, unfortunately, are managed by a team of Nouveaus, so much of it has fallen apart, and what remains is not very Fairho.

...I don't remember Pope's Grocery, but I already wrote that I remember Burkel's. Also La Corona. (I can use that on the Fairho test: How many of the following can you remember: Pope's Grocery, The Central, Comings Hall, Dale's, the Soda Garden, Burkel's, La Corona. Score: Zero to 1: Nouveau. 2 to ALL: Fairho)

Hey, this could be a book! Want to collaborate? I'm serious! Think on all this, and write soon!

Love,
Mary Lois

October 2, 1994

Dear Mary Lois:

Hey, you are really something! I restrained myself from writing back at once, but now that I look at over a month I realize that I am pushing my luck on waiting too long. In the matter of Proust et al., good lord, we have become even more intertwined.

As you probably don't know, I finished Birmingham-Southern in 1950. I was top of the crop and got a teaching fellowship to Tulane. But one day while playing Monopoly with my brother and Sonny Evans in Fairhope I got a call from the Rockefeller Foundation that I had a scholarship to anywhere I wanted to go. I chose Harvard and indeed ended up there. I got there woefully inadequate. Not only had I not read Proust, I had not read Joyce and Mann (They had a course at Harvard called "Proust, Joyce, and Mann"). I didn't qualify for anything, since I had only made it through the first 25 pages (and the last orgasmic pages) of *Ulysses* and some short stories of Mann, including *Death in Venice*.

But then I had not read all that much Dickens or Thackeray or Fielding or anybody. I entered Harvard with utter foreboding, but, unbelievably, classmates kept emerging who had not read all those people either. I stuck it out and kept brandishing all-American writers like Melville, Poe, Twain, and Whitman. I won enough to be remembered at Harvard, but I was stimulated to read beyond my interests. So I have read my way into Proust. I have read a lot of Mann. Joyce is still a disaster as far as I am concerned. So at Harvard I was a skulking kind of evader who kept praying that nobody would discover me. In the process, though, I picked up a bunch of people I didn't much know before—like Wallace Stevens, Henry James, Lafcadio Hearn, William Faulkner, and a bunch of fascinating minor poets.

Your emotional life folds into a kind of stage life. Your recital of all the problems sounded like movements on a stage. I don't mean to consign all this to a kind of dress rehearsal, but the way you wrote it makes it look like something from Ibsen. I wish you could have known King Benton. She was a master of stagedom. She could walk through a room and let everyone in there know exactly his or her role in her life.

14

She could go to the stove (stage right), downstage (the door to the living room), and then cross to stage left (the table). The business, as she called it, might have been as simple as serving spaghetti. The effect was that even her real, often unhappy, life seemed like blocking in scenes for an upcoming performance...

I have thought of buying in Fairhope "for the last countdown" (shudder), but I am put off because of the prices...I like older houses, like 102 N. Bayview. Now I'd put my ass on the line for that one. The house in TBT belonged to a Mrs. Ives, and it was right on the bluff. As you proceeded along Bayview toward town, it was on the right not far beyond the gully that ate its way up from the beach. You never could quite see the whole house, since a drive went off of Bayview...

Love your distinction between Nouveaus and Fairhos...but the Fairhos, I'm not sure there are that many around any more. I moved back for two years in 1963–5, and many had gone by then. The secret of Fairhos was that they respected privacy and kept out of controversies. You could live next door to someone for years and not really know them. Alexis Ferm was a good example. He lived on Summit near the Gastons. He was a mathematician of international importance, but nobody really knew. Winifred Duncan was an important sculptor in her day. The Nouveaus are the really unchanging ones. There will always be a bunch of Nouveaus. I guess I was even one of them, even though I had got sand in my diaper in the late '20s, for I invaded the status quo in 1947 and brought different perspectives.

Fairho quiz? Got every one of your quiz. Do mine: Brumfield's, Pinequat, Price's, Armistead florist, Gooden Real Estate, Parker House, Fairhope Ave. Post Office, Creamery, Moyer's, and a bunch I can't remember but can see as I walk in memory abound the streets.

...Yes, I knew about the Colonial Inn. God, I wish I could have bought that place. I was in Fairhope in time to take pictures of its final weeks. I have some great pictures. I think the area should be enshrined. We never stayed there, but my aunt used to, and once or twice I ate there with her. It was a haunted marvelous place that should have been preserved because of its unique personality among elegant old hotels in the Deep South...

Take care. And let's do work on a book.

Love,
Bob

Robert E. Bell died in October 1999 in Davis, California, of complications after a head injury.

Fairhope Places

"Uptown," Fairhope Avenue in the 1930s

Introduction

This was it, then, the end for roads in Moss Bayou, not-quite-forgotten place, not-quite-remembered road. He turned onto an avenue of magnolias and old heavy houses brooding a thousand mysteries, not-telling houses almost hidden...a breeze unsettled the tree-caught afternoon, shifting the day to new meanings. Then by a simple intuition, Peter knew he had arrived.

Robert E. Bell
The Butterfly Tree, 1959

THE "MOSS BAYOU" of young Bob Bell's novel was a fictional-ized Fairhope. He perceived it as a lazy, lovely Alabama town with special magic bestowed by Mobile Bay glistening at its side. It was that, yet it was more. Fairhope in the 1950s was offbeat, artistic, writerly, unusually varied for a village with a population of three thousand in the Deep South.

The "more" became the mystery for Bell, whose novel spun a tale of people who sought a magical answer to life's meaning, symbolized by a butterfly tree. The "more" is the spirit of Fairhope, which lies just beneath the town's casual charm. Fairhope barely conceals its para-doxical Northern orientation within genteel Southern surroundings.

This spirit was my reality as I grew from a ten-year-old child into a young woman, nurtured by this enlightened little enclave. Fairhope fostered a different way of looking at things, whether one was a Single-Taxer, an educator, a writer, a scientist, an artist, or simply an ordinary person seeking an extraordinary life.

Fairhope's history provided a backdrop for a complex cast of characters. Founded by nineteenth-century idealists who were committed to the institutionalization of social economist Henry George's principles of Single Tax, the town Fairhope was planned as a project to change the world and contribute to the betterment of mankind in the century to come. George's book *Progress and Poverty* inspired Progressives in the nation in the late 1800s, including an Iowa newspaperman named Ernest B. Gaston. He led a group who felt that Henry George's philosophy deserved a demonstration—a Utopia. The club formally incorporated as the Fairhope Industrial Association before they moved here from Des Moines in 1894. The Association's name, based on a remark that such an experiment had a "fair hope of success," came to be the name they chose for the new settlement.

Henry George believed that land should be common property in a community rather than owned by individuals who could trade it at whatever price they chose. He saw great wealth alongside grinding poverty as an evil that could be remedied by the abolition of private land ownership. Although George himself did not favor a Utopian community demonstrating his vision, those 28 people who bought almost four square miles of nearly-useless land they were to call Fairhope in the late 1800s were determined to prove that his idea was sound.

Their wholehearted belief in a wildly impractical notion became the beginning of an unconventional little town for anywhere in America, let alone southeastern Alabama. After a shaky beginning, Fairhope in the early twentieth century became a place where free thinkers were permitted to act on their thoughts.

Another factor in the town's growth and appeal to intellectuals and radical thinkers was the new educational system put forth by Marietta Johnson, destined to become an internationally known educator. She was a schoolteacher who moved to Fairhope in 1907. Having been a teacher of teachers in Minnesota, she had a great dream. She founded a grammar school that came to be called The School of Organic Education.

Her theory, which she hoped would change the educational systems in this country and throughout the world, was that education is organic to life; in fact, she felt that the words "education" and "life" were synonyms.

The Organic School, in its heyday in the early 1920s, was a center of much activity in the town, bringing together people who contributed creative ideas as they carved out new lives. They filled the town with adventurous children who attended a school designed to change the world. A special synergy between the Single Tax Colony and the school was the ephemeral connection at Fairhope's heart.

The town had a Bohemian aura in those days. Founded on an economic premise, isolated, and peopled by iconoclasts, Fairhope was unusual at best. In the 1920s the townspeople, under the direction of a noted Shakespearean scholar from the Chicago area, appeared in productions of the Bard's plays in annual festivals. Near town during this period there was also a nudist colony—said to be for health and fitness—and many locals and visitors went there for brief visits. Those who were children at the time are elderly ladies now, and most are vague as to exactly what the place was, if they speak of it at all.

Fairhope was a place where progressive thinkers came together in mutual respect—intellectually motley and philosophically varied though they were. By its very nature, Fairhope was a town that cele-brated diversity while it lived its own vision.

This laid the background for succeeding generations, although inevitably Fairhope's commitment to its original purpose and its economic mission waned as the town grew. By the time Bob Bell and I hit town—separately, and of different generations—just a memory of those transcendent days remained. However, its unusual origins, and perhaps a collective memory of those pioneer Single-Taxers, may have attracted the remarkable people who drifted into Fairhope in the mid-twentieth century.

Fairhope was a world apart in the quiet days from its visionary birth through the gently eccentric years of the late 1950s. Due to the chaotic growth the community is experiencing a hundred years after its founding it is changing rapidly, and yet its past is still seductive. Like the young searcher in Bob's book, many find that past hard to let go.

> He didn't want to leave, because the butterfly tree, the tree that was the beginning and end for all the people who had come to have meaning for him, was starting to be something else, and this time he wasn't certain what. He backed away, and when he got to the steps it was still there, fully visible. He walked up the steps backward, making it last, for with all the unknowns about butterfly trees and their searchers, he wasn't sure it would ever be again, especially as now.
>
> Robert E. Bell, Ibid.

Bob Bell—Fairhope in the 1930s

SUMMER IN TARRANT CITY came to mean out of-school since, even from the first summer after the first grade, summer meant freedom from shoes, freedom from hurrying not to be tardy. Summer meant woods and creek, cousins, wiener roasts, and library books. Sometimes it meant rainy days when we had to play on the old front porch, which was a kind of huge umbrella from under which we watched the cars swishing past on Pinson Street and people running to get under shelter. In the summer we played games of jacks, and we drew pictures with crayons; we played softball in the vacant lot behind Hill's grocery store; we had rubber-gun battles, and a few fights with bloody noses. Every Saturday we went ritually to the Imperial Theater to see Westerns, "chapter pictures," and animated cartoons.

But the main thing that summer came to mean was the possibility of Fairhope.

Fairhope, a small town on the Eastern Shore of Mobile Bay, became over a period of time the ultimate dream place, a kind of Emerald City. A nirvana. Yet it was none of these as much as a place of sensual fulfillment after weeks of hot city pavements and empty afternoons of the sameness of Pinson Street and Wharton Avenue.

No number of plunges into Five Mile Creek could equal one ecstatic drop into the green waters of Mobile Bay.

It had started when I was a mere baby. There is an old saying in Fairhope that once you get its sand in your shoes you can never really leave it. I was taken to Fairhope as a baby and hung up on a cypress limb in one of those springy baby seats. So I undoubtedly got sand in my diaper—far more compelling, I am sure, than mere sand in shoes.

Our 1934 trip in the old Essex had established forever the blue-print for all the trips to follow, and we had already mounted favorite spots and sensations in our memories. Even the landmarks along the long route, Highway 31, were lovingly anticipated—counties, towns, rivers with sibilant names, the first appearance of Spanish moss, the pine trees with turpentine cups, signs that warned, "Livestock at Large."

We usually left well before daybreak in order to be across the two mountains and well down the highway by sunup. Today our old car would not be expected to make it to the first shopping center; but on our side was the fact that Daddy was a mechanic.

We set our sights on places with magic names like Calera, Verbena, Alabaster. We looked forward to Jemison and Thorsby. Then came Clanton. Montgomery was next, with its bridge over the Alabama River, and immediately Spanish moss started appearing. This bridge represented a crossing from one world into another. We got to Greenville, Georgiana, McKenzie, Evergreen. Finally to Brewton, where the highway angled west, and we were rather in the home stretch. Then came Flomaton, on the Florida line; then Atmore, running all the time beside the L&N railway line. Bay Minette would have brought us safely into Baldwin County, but we didn't quite make it, since night had arrived. We stopped in a rundown tourist court, had a supper of kidney beans, and slept. Mother was nervous about the owner, since she was sure he was a drunk. He made howling noises during the night that rather supported her suspicions.

We arose early, had breakfast, and made for Bay Minette. (It should be said that the roadside coffee Daddy made in an open pot over a fire, drunk from tin cups, was nectar of the gods. Having drunk coffee since the cradle, we were good judges.) Bay Minette was kind of a doorway to the final stage of our long journey. It was the county seat, and we skirted the tidy courthouse in the still-sleeping town and reveled over palmettos and occasional stretches of white sand that betokened things to come. From then on was the dream country, the land of rising and setting suns, the land where times could have no stop and there was no disappointment.

Here there were creeks with black, white, and ocher bottoms visible through clear water. There were trees that drooped a burden of brooding and mysterious moss toward the ground. Here were pine needles carpeting the ground. Here were turpentine cups sucking tall and proud pines, and here were cattle roaming at large in this free and leisurely world.

Sunlight had a special quality, and probably the greatest sensual experience of my life was the supreme moment at one special spot on the highway at Spanish Fort. A round of a curve, a certain elevation, and then there was the sparkle of sunlight on Mobile Bay like a thousand diamonds down the long hill. There was a cheer then and cheers in later times, a cheer that has really never stopped.

When we got to Fairhope, we sometimes stayed at the Casino, a huge, lumbering rather dilapidated building at the beginning of the Big Wharf, since there was nowhere else we could afford. We got two rooms there for fifty cents a night each. We ate on the beach, of course, and food never tasted so good. There were bacon and eggs and the wonderful coffee. There were pimiento cheese sandwiches. Best of all, there were freshly caught fish. Even plain old bread tasted like a special manna from heaven.

One year we didn't stay at the Casino, but in a waterfront cabin in the Fairhope bayfront area known as Nicholsville. A Mrs. Georgia

Nichols had about a dozen cottages along the highway, on the cliffside and at water level. These were rented at super-reasonable prices, usually by the week, to families or groups. They all had names, which was a thrill to us, since we could put these exotic names in our memory for reliving the experiences of the trip. The cottage we got, Sandy Ridge, was one of three or four on the water, the end one toward the Big Wharf, and on one side was a marshland full of vines, tall grass, birds, lizards, and certainly snakes. The cliff rose behind, atop which sat another row of cottages. Giant magnolias rose behind the beach cottages, and one of them supported a kind of tree house reached by a long flight of wooden steps. The beach in front was in its natural state, with driftlogs, dried seaweed, clumps of tall golden grass, sandspurs, and interesting debris that had washed ashore. From the front door a wooden walkway crossed the spongy ground to the beach. To the left, past the other two cottages, a rather tumbledown little wharf reached out a hundred yards or so.

Sandy Ridge was sparsely furnished. We had brought our own linen to make up the two or three double beds, which were not meant to be comfortable. A few chairs and odds and ends of tables and chests were about it. Light came from low-watt bulbs that hung down in the center of the room. There were big closets, and from them came an indefinable odor. It was like vanilla flavoring and the smell of the wood of the wharves in the hot sun. The kitchen area had a plain long unpainted wooden table with attached backless benches. An old-fashioned sink, an icebox, and an oil stove completed the basic needs. There was no hot water. A shower stall, side by side with a toilet, afforded the sanitary facilities. No luxury hotel in the world could have pleased us more, since the rustic nature of the cottages became part of the pervasive mystique of Fairhope. We unloaded our stuff and started to explore.

First, we had to swim. That is what we had waited for. We went out on the little wharf in front of the beach cottages. A set of steps led into the water. We soon found, though, to our dismay, that the Nicholsville area was not good for swimming. The bottom was mucky, and there were beds of seaweed that probably harbored all manner of unwelcome creatures. We were forced to tread the bottom, since we couldn't swim. A few older kids didn't seem to mind and splashed in and out of the water. The end of the pier had a number of compartments for changing clothes, and they created a kind of maze. You could go into one of them and make your way through an opening to a platform just above water level. It was fun to swing around underneath where the waves hit the pilings and watch the barnacles reach out of their razor-sharp burrows for the microscopic food that came their way. You could see fish, too, when the water was clear— darting schools of minnows and now and then something bigger.

My brother Sonny was fifteen, so he found different things to interest him. Mrs. Nichols had two daughters, Alice and Madelyn. They came every afternoon to the wharf and swam. Alice was blonde and pretty and, like all the other Fairhope kids, could swim and dive with what seemed to be a formulaic precision. Sonny was shy, so nothing ever came of his fascination.

The Big Wharf was our ultimate destination. That's where the real swimming was. That's where you could walk out and look back at the shoreline that reached from the red bluff on the north to a spit of land that reached out south of Nicholsville, after which came two other magic stretches called Battles Wharf and Point Clear. God really knew what He was doing when He created the Eastern Shore. The Big Wharf started, of course, at the Casino, which had long been incorporated into our memory archive. We regarded it fondly each time we passed, forgetting the claustrophobic rooms and the mosquitoes. Stepping onto the Big Wharf for the first time on each trip was like returning to a long lost spiritual refuge. It changed a little each time we came back to it. Early on, it had had wide wooden tracks for driving autos out to the ferries. By now they were gone. On our last trip, there had been a high slide for swimmers. Now it was gone, too, and a rather weatherbeaten old two-storied bathhouse remained. Beyond were the familiar sheds, and on either side of the wharf steps led down to platforms for swimmers. From each platform a ladder descended into the water. Across a short expanse were floating platforms, also with short ladders.

As far as we were concerned, this was as far as one needed to go, but the wharf extended far beyond. At a point some one hundred yards beyond, there was another platform on the north side. Then a long expanse got you to the end of the wharf, which broadened out and betokened the old ferry days. Little by little, though, the end of the pier was falling into decay and had taken on a snaggle-toothed appearance, with naked pilings sticking up. There had been a fire or two.

But sunbathers still came to the end, and net-casters brought in catches of writhing, silvery mullet. At night the expanse was lighted, and pole fishers silently dropped their weighted lines. Pop Bell was in paradise. I might say here that my grandfather's fishing enthusiasm was rewarded. He caught many, and as unusual as it might sound, we had fish for breakfast the whole time we were there. To this day, I cannot imagine a more elegant breakfast than fried fish, eggs, pancakes, bacon, grits, coffee, and toast.

We swam, descending by the ladders into the water. We couldn't negotiate the fullness of the early morning tide, so when afternoon came we were there. So was the youthful population of Fairhope. They were young gods and goddesses, golden and joyous. The bathing suits had changed. On the last trip, boys still wore tops—shirts with a carved-out opening under the armpits—but by this time that uniform had disappeared, and naked chests were the rule. Girls still wore one-piece suits that descended an inch or so on the thighs, but there were no little skirts attached. Bathing caps were not used by these golden creatures.

The luxury of the velvety water was almost unreal. We were creek kids and knew gravel bottoms and coaxing currents. We had to adjust each time to the undulations of waves, the getting in and out of the water by slippery and barnacled ladders, the jumping off platforms, the footing on sandy bottoms. Whatever we needed to learn, we were willing students. The one thing we most needed to learn was how to swim.

Things were made more interesting, if that was possible, by the appearance of another Tarrant City family, who moved into an adjacent cottage. These were the Gudgenses. They had a little girl about Billy's age named Emma Lou, and we wasted no time in becoming very good friends in the way that kids do. The Gudgenses settled in, and Billy and I, with our superior knowledge of Fairhope, set about to introduce all our favorite things to Emma Lou. She was a sweet little girl, destined for lifelong plainness, with a kind of twisted little smile and a somewhat comic aspect. In her red bathing suit trimmed in white, she accompanied us into the tree house, where we tried to think of ways to weave pine needles and use the red-seeded magnolia cones to some kind of advantage. We traipsed the beach in front of the cottages, looking for treasures that had come in with the tide. We went out on the Nicholses' pier. We accompanied our beer-drinking fathers to Burkel's, a kind of pavilion south of Nicholsville. In Burkel's there was a long counter and a wide floor for dancing. It overhung the water, and from the bar you could look across to Mobile. Burkel was a dark-visaged man who welcomed one and all. Daddy, Pop, and Ray Gudgens drank long and deep while Billy, Emma Lou, and I waited to be taken from this adult place back to the world we knew how to deal with. One deal was a little snack stand just beyond Nicholsville on the highway. We discovered cream sodas there, a sickish kind of vanilla-flavored soda pop; and they also had root beer, chocolate Nehis, and a variety of other things. The Casino had the same things, but we couldn't get to the Big Wharf without adult accompaniment, so we had to make do with the little stand. Forevermore we determined that cream sodas were an invention of Fairhope, no matter if they might have been introduced in New York or Timbuktu.

There was also the beach north of the Casino to show Emma Lou. This was, after all, the part of Fairhope that I knew from sand-in-the-diaper days. A sand road ran along the bottom of the cliff. On the left lay the narrow strip of beach, and beyond it sandbars mysteriously appeared and disappeared. Gulls hung on wind currents and dropped suddenly to the water surface. Boats drifted up and down, tugging at moorings to posts. A couple of little piers went out a few yards. Then you went under a canopy of trees, with a jungle of twisted vines to your right and cleared areas with wooden tables and benches to your left. The road snaked among trees to come finally to an open area, where there was a pump for water. And here was the wonderful Little Wharf that ended about a hundred yards out with a covered platform for swimmers. At its beginning was a crystal-clear spring that came from under tree roots and spread into the Bay. We showed Emma Lou how to dam it up and keep it that way for up to half an hour. We introduced her to the paths that led into the thicket behind. We walked as far as we thought the road went, since it curved around and came back. A more primitive road went on, but we had never dared take it.

After the world of the waterfront, Billy and I took Emma Lou uptown. Walking from Nicholsville, you crossed the dizzying height of the gully by the Colonial Inn and then turned right on the street that ended at the Big Wharf. Oh, the houses of Fairhope along this way! They were Mediterranean colors, and we envied the people who lived in them. Across Fairhope Avenue on the left was a vast area carpeted with pine needles. Nothing was there, but it rose to a kind of pinnacle in the middle. Someone told us later that it was an Indian burial mound.

So we went on up the street. The first real landmark was Moyer's Drugstore. This was a drugstore like no other we had ever known.

There were imaginative things there. Maybe not, really, but it had something we might have thought of as "Fairhopeness." Dr. Moyer was a kindly man and never seemed worried about our presence. I think that year we bought a box of rubber bands of various colors.

We walked on up the street, past more houses, and came to the main part of town. Here was a movie theatre. And then there were other businesses. The street was lined with palmettos.

The end of our tour was at the Creamery. Here you could buy ice cream in exotic flavors. We had experienced orange-pineapple and rainbow before, but they had other flavors, too. Buildings nearby were said to be the Organic School, but we didn't have time to wonder about that. We licked our cones and walked back the way we had come.

This was another trip to Fairhope that firmed up our adoration of the place. We looked at the sunning demigods and goddesses on the Big Wharf, we plunged around in the clear green waters, we reveled in the sun-dappled upper beach, and we experienced the everyday world of "uptown."

We tried to imagine what it would be to live in such surroundings. But, as always, the time finally came to leave. Each time this happened, I left part of myself there. To me there could be no idea of heaven more perfect. Heaven could even turn out to be a bore, but Fairhope never could be. I was totally convinced of this.

Uptown

GHOSTS CONSTANTLY CONFRONT ME IN FAIRHOPE. Vivid
memories of people from former days, buildings as they once
were, little objects now missing, long-gone businesses, they all
flood my consciousness. I see the old even as I am looking at the new—
the storefronts now occupied by up-to-date boutiques and trendy retail
shops. It's almost like being in two places at the same time.

Sometimes in Fairhope I can look at a perfectly solid building and
find I can move it back and forth in time. (You may have had a similar
experience. A beloved face transformed by years soon becomes in your
eyes just as it once was—the elder face through memory becomes its
youthful self).

Fairhopers always used to refer to the business district as "Uptown."
It was not an affectation to say, "I'm going uptown now," referring to
the town center. I read something about Iowa recently that referred to
the Iowa custom of calling the center of town "uptown" rather than
"downtown." It would seem that this is where the expression came
from—its first settlers, from Iowa.

This usage seems to have passed into history, and indeed Fairhope
is the only place where I have run into it. When my late friend Jerry
Newell and I lived in New York, she still had the Fairhope habit of

referring to shopping and running errands as "going uptown." When Jerry would announce that she had to "go uptown" on Saturday, her New York friends would respond, "Really? What do you have to do in Harlem?"

I can explain some of what I see. You might find this interesting.

One favorite place, and an ideal one to begin the time travel, is at Fairhope Avenue and School Street, on what is now the Fairhope campus of Faulkner State Community College. When I am there today, I seem to hear teenagers laughing, talking, and teasing—just as they did in the early 1950s when I was a little kid, looking up at them. On that much-changed corner, I am transported to the old Organic School campus, facing the Recreation Hall, long since renovated and renamed Dahlgren Hall.

A few pine trees remain, but they were smaller when the Fairhope High School boys like Jimmy Anderson, Richard Macon, Mike Ponder, or Billy Scott would wait on their bicycles as Organic School events ended, hoping to walk the girls home or wait with them while their parents came to pick them up if they lived as far away as Montrose. I was one of those who lived in Montrose, and had that miraculous thing, an older sister whom those boys were interested in, giving me a glimpse of what was to come. Those evenings echo in my mind, nights with warm winds, lightning bugs, adolescent tensions, and my own yearning —to *be* adolescent. We were learning conversation, socialization, and flirtation. Surely teenaged girls are as pretty now, the boys as eager, the conversation as awkward.

The Fairhope Creamery was just down Fairhope Avenue toward the Big Wharf. Mr. Berglin, whose son Robert was my age, owned the Creamery. The Creamery sold big ice blocks, and produced Azalea Ice Cream (which contained no floral additives).

Fairhope's ice cream was famous—and had been so since the early Colony days. Visitors loved the frozen treat, made from cream from country cows, sold at one point from the creamery at the beach—said to be the first ice cream factory in Alabama. Every visitor headed for Fairhope's ice cream, served in the old-fashioned waffle cones.

A blacksmith's shack stood next to the Creamery. The man worked with his anvil and fire, forging horseshoes and other iron pieces, to fill a need for farmers and equestrians, and providing a historic picture, right on up into the 1950s.

Back on the Organic side of the street, Comings Hall was just about where the Faulkner administration building now stands. Comings Hall was a wonderful old building, with wooden floors perfect for folk dancing and a good-sized stage with ample dressing rooms and good acoustics. The plain building had exposed beams and wooden posts, with a comfortable, old-wood smell. Students at the school, with much assistance from the community, had built the hall in 1916. They named it for Samuel H. and Lydia Comings, early benefactors and staunch supporters of Marietta Johnson.

In the 1950s, Comings Hall was still solid, but had the dilapidated look of many buildings and cottages on Organic's campus. I remember it as a place where special events took place, dressed up for Spring Festival with batik banners made in Arts & Crafts class by the high school students who had graduated before us; its stage flanked with magnolia leaves and blossoms for graduation ceremonies. The school, the Fairhope Little Theatre, and touring groups used the hall for plays. It was also a venue for parties, basketball games, and events throughout the school year.

Previous Fairhopers had used the building for civic meetings, movies, lectures, and dances that the whole town attended. As a civic center, Comings Hall was the heart of town. Although it was long past its prime, and we Organic students often complained about its condition, memory has almost immortalized it for me, and I realize that since its destruction no building has truly replaced it.

Across Bancroft Street is a sandwich shop and next to it a laundry. The latter was there when I grew up and still operates, definitely under new management, and, recently relocated and renovated, it looks quaintly in keeping with the new façades. Dale's, across the street, where the busy Julwin's Restaurant is now, was a dark place with vinyl booths. A rather forlorn little bar, Dale's took on life when groups such as casts from the Little Theatre productions met there after rehearsals (in Comings Hall), for talk over beer.

Dale's' neighbor, now a conglomeration of shops where one can buy comestibles, antiques, and gifts, was at that time the Gaston Motor Company, run by E. B. Gaston's descendants. Gaston had been the original scribe and town founder.

Above loomed a water tower, identifying Fairhope for all who passed. This was Fairhope before its corners spilled forth flowers, before its sidewalks were paved and bordered in brick—a little town, plain and gentle, unselfconscious, unassuming. It was not bland, however; nor was it bleak as many small Southern towns were. It was not split down its center by a railroad track dividing the "haves" from the "have-nots." Fairhope had a layout unlike many towns its size—no central square flanked or centered by official buildings. It was dappled with green areas: trees here and there, often palm, magnolia, or oak, planted randomly rather than in the measured, manicured manner preferred today.

The original wooden water tower stood at the psychological center of town—in the intersection of Fairhope Avenue and Section Street. In the early 1900s adventurous youngsters climbed up there for a bird's eye view of town, just to say they'd done it. One elderly lady explained, "There wasn't much to do in Fairhope in those days."

A dry goods company always resided where Wilkin's now stands. I remember two previous incarnations on the site: Brumfield's and Bedsole's. These establishments carried the basic garments that outfitted Fairhope before the many boutiques that now line its streets. This corner was the location for the original general store, run by the Mershon brothers. Henry Crawford, whose granddaughter was in my

Organic School class and whose namesake grandson is still in the community, later operated the store. In the 1920s the store was operated by the original Ike Pitman, whose family still live in Fairhope.

On the southeastern corner, where a women's sportswear boutique now stands, was Wheeler Mercantile, operated as a general store by Felix Beiser and Ralph Young, which sold everything from groceries to farm implements. In my teenage years, the spot was McKean's Hardware—an old-fashioned hardware store that smelled of rubber tires and sold assorted household items.

Across Section Street was the Fairhope Pharmacy, which still stands. In the 1950s the Pharmacy had a soda fountain that served hand-squeezed lemonade along with fountain Cokes and milkshakes made the old-fashioned way, with fresh milk and ice cream. A sign on the new Pharmacy says, "No food or drink allowed inside."

The town dentist's office was upstairs in that building.

The Bank of Fairhope was next, formal with its columns, yet Fairhope-casual inside. Next to it was teen-age heaven, the Soda Garden. The Soda Garden abutted the Fairhope dime store, known as "Shell Stores," a typical five-and-dime replete with trinkets, ribbons, notions, and seasonal specialties such as valentines and Halloween decorations.

The *Fairhope Courier* offices were nearby, where Miss Frankie (Frances Gaston Crawford), twinkly and busy, had inherited the job of editor when her father died. She operated the paper on the premise that editing a weekly newspaper did not require altering news items submitted. She seemed to view the *Courier* as a creative-writing endeavor for the community, sometimes with hilarious results.

Miss Frankie was my Organic classmate Sally Crawford's grandmother, and it was our class joke, with more than a grain of truth, that if we wondered what Sally had been up to the previous weekend, we could pick up the *Courier* on Thursday and find out. News notes included old-fashioned phrases such as, "Miss Sally Crawford motored to New Orleans to visit her charming cousins over the weekend."

Any item submitted to the *Courier* was run without editing, and without question. Miss Frankie was much admired by locals, and they loved nothing more about her than the way she filled the paper with everyday Fairhope. She would get on the telephone on Monday morning and call everybody in town to find out what had happened over the weekend that she might use in the next Thursday's edition.

The bench in front of the *Courier* office was usually occupied by a man named George who never wore shoes, summer or winter. He was almost toothless and had large, ugly feet that were always dirty and looked tough as leather, but he was a nice enough man, known by everybody. George raised enormous tortoises where he lived—near what is now the Eastern Shore Art Center, on the gully's edge.

The Colony Shop then stood across the street. Verona Beiser and a business partner ran it. Verona had a Nina Foch look, with long blonde hair swept into a chignon, and she dressed in the clothes The Colony Shop sold; she was a svelte walking advertisement. The shop then occupied two floors in the building that is now a gift shop below and William Richmond's architectural office on the second story.

On the other side of the street, next to the retail store, was the Pinequat Shop, a Fairhope original. This little shop, fragrant with pungent spices, had been run by Anna Bellangee Call and her daughter Helen since Fairhope's early days. The name for the shop was taken from their best-selling items—kumquat marmalade put up in jars enclosed in pine and raffia baskets. Anna and Helen Call sold handmade gifts, such as necklaces made from chinaberries, Spanish moss dyed in colors, and unusual items like ivory Buddhas (for $1 apiece), and their customers came back again and again.

There was a bakery, which I remember being run by the Knobloch family, and Kamper's Newsstand, later owned by the enterprising Gavin Hunter. What is now the *Courier* office was built as the

Fairhope Post Office, a gathering place where people awaited their mail before there was home delivery.

There was another pharmacy next to it, Holland Pharmacy, which is now a gift shop operated by Brenny's. Near the corner, in the building now occupied by the Old Bay Pub, was the popular Central Café, owned by Mr. and Mrs. Oliviere ("olive-ear"). The hardware store always stood on the corner—at least as far back as I can remember.

There was, in the 1950s, a photographer's office up the street, and one occupied the same spot up until very recently.

Fairhope's real center for me in the 1950s was next door to that photographer. The Fairhope Theatre faced Fairhope Avenue at the corner of Church Street.. Family films ran every day. There was a 3:15 P.M. show Monday through Friday for the school crowd, and Mr. Summerlin, the owner, mailed a printed calendar to everyone in town every month. We could then plan our movie-going schedules for a month in advance. I probably attended movies two or three times a week after school, usually with a few friends in tow.

My attachment to movies was stronger than most. This was brought home to me many years later in a recollection told me by Linda Horne, whose parents were well-known intellectuals in town. Linda said her mother had not been exposed to movies as a girl and always felt she was missing something as a result. She didn't want to deny this world to her children, so she didn't discourage Linda when I would invite her to go to a movie with me.

There were times when Linda and I would take the Greyhound bus to Mobile, see a movie at a big downtown theatre within walking distance of the bus station, and then get on the next bus home, chatting about movies all the way there and back.

Years later Linda, driving home to Housatonic, Connecticut, from Boston, saw an attractive, middle-aged couple in intense conversation, walking on a roadside path. They looked familiar to her, and she kept saying to herself, "I used to know those people; they're friends of Mary Lois's," but she couldn't place them. Try as she might, their names didn't come to her.

As she pulled into her driveway she remembered the names of my "friends": Paul Newman and Joanne Woodward.

The A&W Root Beer was across Church Street from the Fairhope Theater. This had been the location of one of Fairhope's early businesses, a gas station known as "Mecca Station." Remodeled with Victorian trim, it has seen many transformations.

Another gas station facing it on Fairhope Avenue, once run by Prince Griffin, has been a shop for years now. I remember Mr. Griffin, who had a heart attack at a young age, when I look at the changes time has wrought on this corner. Prince would have enjoyed Barbara, the "Tomato Lady," selling produce from her truck between his station and the hardware store, but I don't know what he'd make of the rest of town.

Down the hill businesses thinned, and little beachy houses dotted either side of Fairhope Avenue. The Mershon family still lived in the big house on the corner of Summit Street that became a bed and breakfast called "Mershon Court." Moyer's Drugstore was at Summit and Fairhope, too. Then there were houses with names, like "Kanuck," built and named by the McCoy family who came to the area from Canada. Like many similar houses, Kanuck operated as a hotel in years past.

At the bottom of the street, facing the south end of Knoll Park, stood the pale green apartment building then known as PATLYNN. At that time the PATLYNN looked *very* 1940s, with a square, blocky design and glass bricks for light in the front hall. It has been updated now with the leaded glass doors so stylish in the 1990s and balconies offering views of the Bay and surrounding parks.

A pleasant wooden building known as the Red Cross Building once stood on the bluff where the monument to Henry George now is.

It was used for all kinds of meetings in addition to those of the Red Cross, including the Eastern Shore Art Association.

Today you can still find a bench here at sunset or just stand and breathe the air carrying the mood that is the soul of Fairhope. The beauty of this spot inspired the original settlers and still looks much the same. Its pines, its breezes, its access to the uniquely Fairhope view of the Bay, will always be our link to those idealistic hearts and purposeful minds of the town's past.

Bob Bell with little brother, Billy,
at the Fairhope beach, circa 1936

Bob Bell—A Setting for Memories

FAIRHOPE. You can be there and still be homesick for Fairhope. This is not simply nostalgia for the good old days but a wistful recall of whole eras that gave Fairhope a special flavor and put together time and place in an almost inextricable relationship. For those of us who came and went over half a century, this quality has given the town a mystique unavailable in places that merely changed with the times.

My family came to Fairhope on trips from the early thirties to the late forties. Childhood and adolescence happened during these years. Fairhope Avenue offered new experiences each year. Restaurants and other business enterprises came and went. Palmettos once lined the streets. The Bay glistened down the hill. There were always the unchangeables, like Moyer's Drugstore, the Creamery, the Organic School buildings, the Bank with its white columns, the Corte House. And, of course, there was the Indian mound, the beach with its seeping springs, and the gullies. We came to understand that one year's Fairhope did not always equal the next. But the changes were subtle enough that we had no trouble incorporating them into our experience.

The Big Wharf, as we called it, changed. The old wooden runway for automobiles loading on the ferry out to the end eventually was dismantled. A huge old bathhouse fell into disrepair. A slide for swimmers was torn down. The Casino underwent a series of facelifts. But the eternal element of the whole wharf scene was the incredibly beautiful young people who came every day to sun and swim. Bathing suit styles changed, but the sunners and swimmers did not. They were the beautiful people of Fairhope. As an adolescent finally I came to regard them as creatures from the pages of mythology. They were as slim as sea creatures and agile and alive. I would watch them shake themselves and walk to the edge of the wooden platforms and then knife into the water in dives that barely disturbed the surface. I used to wonder how it would be to share a classroom with them, to know what they thought about; and I longed to have my family move to Fairhope.

That was not to be for many years yet to come. In fact, I had finished high school and even part of college before we finally did move to Fairhope. I remembered the wharf and its bounty of beautiful people, and I wondered where they had gone. Where indeed did stunning water creatures go after they stroked the distances between swims, dried off, and went back up the Casino hill?

It wasn't too long before I discovered the Soda Garden. That's where the latest generation of the magnificent wharf people went. This oasis was next to the Bank, and here everyone stopped at least once a day to see what was happening. The Soda Garden was a narrow area next to the corner drugstore, and down one side were booths. Soda fountain concoctions were the principal stock, but one could also get hamburgers and other varieties of what we later called junk food.

The Soda Garden's clientele was not limited, however, to the young crowd. Little kids came in with their mothers and fathers. Older people stopped in. I myself, not too long out of military service, came by almost every day and certainly after picking up my veteran's unemployment check at the Legion Club every Tuesday morning.

During that first summer of living in Fairhope I also became involved in a play called *Out of the Frying Pan*, and its cast was mainly young people recently out of high school and two or three home for the summer from college—Raymond and Peggy Wood, Al Barton, Patsy Porter, Dicky Dryer. Bill Gray, an older man, had a leading role. We would meet at the Soda Garden after rehearsal, and I knew that I had met at least a few of the swimmers from years before. With their clothes on they were like ordinary people, but you could still sense a kind of naked abandon as if they might be swimming among the barnacled pilings.

The curious thing about the Soda Garden is that I scarcely remember it at all. It was so integrally a part of the Fairhope scene of the time that it blended into the Main Street aspect of things. I think it was there for years, eventually expanding into the drugstore and somehow losing part of its identity. But in this respect it was characteristically a Fairhope institution, one of the verities that moved into being and then gradually out of being. The Soda Garden became in later years a kind of symbol, more or less like the old movie house that also disappeared without any fanfare, like the old post office, like the Pinequat Shop.

But there is no way to remember the Fairhope of the late forties without remembering the Soda Garden. Its passing did not diminish the Fairhope mystique but left instead a kind of warmth in a collective recall.

The Soda Garden

I WAS NINE YEARS OLD. Now that my life has spanned several nine-year periods, I can appreciate how very short a time that is. That brief time had been spent in the city of Mobile, with family summer vacations at the lagoon of Gulf Shores and on the beach at Point Clear.

Mobile had been a difficult place for our little freewheeling family to spend those years. Its big, impersonal red-brick school, its formal social strata, and its urban limits impinged on a child's imagination. Fairhope would be the place where I could grow wings.

Fairhope felt like a vacation, all the time. Nobody was strict; nobody was scared. My parents were more relaxed, and so were we three children.

We were to be enrolled in The School of Organic Education. Whatever trepidation I had was soon dispelled in its casual, child-centered atmosphere. I found myself at the beginning of a happy new time.

The Organic School was more user-friendly than most places, and certainly more than other schools of the day (although the phrase was unknown). At lunch, students could bring a lunch, go home, or eat at the School Home, where boarding students and several of the teachers ate. Or they could eat uptown at any of the few restaurants and sandwich shops within walking distance of the campus.

I would go up Section Street to the bus station coffee shop called "The Sandwich Lounge" where Mr. Behling made hot dogs from real veal sausage, new to the area. He was a jolly gentleman from Chicago whose daughter was in my sister's Junior High class.

My friends and I also went to the Central Café, later the Olde Towne Pub.

Mostly we went to The Soda Garden, which was usually full of teenagers. Movies of the 1940s and '50s often picture the soda shop with a counter, plastic booths and tables, and a Movieola jukebox; a place packed with teenagers in bobby sox. The girls wore plaid skirts with sweaters, saddle oxfords or penny loafers, and boys wore trousers that weren't always blue jeans. These soda shop movie teens jitterbugged, giggled and squealed about the big game or the big dance or whatever was about to happen.

The Soda Garden was a lot like that. It had a jukebox, with "Mule Train," a raucous, noisy attempt at a song by Frankie Laine. Charlie Ingersoll, who was in love with Mary Ann Patterson, used to play it sometimes just to make her mad, since she claimed to hate it, triggering an excuse for a feigned argument that would have to be resolved. Most of the time the jukebox played "You Belong to Me," by Jo Stafford, or Vaughn Monroe's "Ghost Riders in the Sky."

I was one of the younger kids at The Soda Garden, which was run by Ken and Dot Cain, and they were the parents of a boy in my class at Organic.

It was a busy, happy place. I remember a grave little girl named Patty Grey, who went to my school but I hadn't yet met, drinking a delicious pink concoction. She let me taste it. It was the best drink I ever had. Patty told me it was a cherry limeade, but I thought she said, "cherry homemade."

I ordered one myself, a few days later.

"Cherry homemade!" I said firmly.

Mrs. Cain patiently tried to understand what I wanted, since they had no drink by that name. At last, working together, we got it, and I was presented my own cherry limeade. It had a dash of cherry syrup in a tangy limeade mixture on crushed ice in a cone-shaped paper cup in a plastic holder, sipped through a paper straw.

Also on the menu was a Roast Beef Poor Boy, really a hot roast beef sandwich, a childhood favorite of mine, served on a larger bun. I remember it now, warm, soft, beefy, and smothered with gravy.

The first soft ice cream I ever had was at The Soda Garden. A new machine produced what was called a "Frosted Malted," chocolate malt soft ice cream in a paper cup, before Styrofoam had been invented. It was as delicious as it sounds.

In time a man who was in the business of selling electronic equipment bought the Soda Garden. He kept the fountain for a while, but soon the booths were replaced by television sets and hi-fi equipment.

Teenagers frequented the ice cream parlor for several more years, as a hangout after the 3:15 movie ended, but the television sets gradually took over.

Nothing like the Soda Garden has been around since it closed its doors.

Mary Lois Timbes (center), the happiest
modern dancer at Spring Festival, 1951

A Campus of Butterfly Trees

I F THERE REALLY WERE A PLACE where Bob Bell's magical tree with all the secrets to happiness took root in Fairhope, it would have been on the campus of the School of Organic Education. Here children could shake off the responsibilities so often thrust upon them by the adult world. In the supportive atmosphere of this extraordinary school, children were playful, hopeful, optimistic, and ready to learn more each day. I know, because I was one of those children.

I began life in the 1940s in Mobile, Alabama, a slow-moving Southern port with an entrenched social system and schools that adhered to the repressive "old-fashioned discipline" educational theory.

Traditional attitudes marked my first three years of school: The teacher is always right, and you children are a noisy nuisance. I got A's and B's on my report cards, but often came home with a C in "conduct" and a note, "Talks too much," written in teacher-neat handwriting.

When I was nine, my family moved to Montrose, five miles north of Fairhope. My sister, brother, and I looked forward to attending Fairhope's public school. But our father had heard of another school in town. He had spoken with some teenagers who were astonishingly enthusiastic about their school, describing this place where they learned folk dancing and handicrafts along with their academic studies in small classes. What appealed to him most was that the students *liked* going to school.

When told our parents had decided to enroll us in The School of Organic Education, the children next door seized on it as a subject for torment: "Rotten Organic!" Even before we'd entered the school they leveled this heart-chilling jibe. We were going to be outsiders at an age when we yearned for nothing more than acceptance.

I would be attending a school without tests, grades, or rewards for accomplishment. Folk dancing and arts and crafts were required classes; reading wasn't taught to first graders, and we could wear anything we wanted. All these prospects were so radical I really couldn't believe them. I was only nine, accustomed to the strictures taken for granted in that red-brick building in Mobile.

I'll never forget my first day. My class was to be in the Bell Building, and I remember being afraid I would get it wrong: Where on earth was the Bell Building? Mama said, "Maybe that's the building with the bell in it," but I was convinced it couldn't be that simple.

Organic was unlike anything I'd ever experienced. I felt totally unprepared. All I knew was that it was not one big brick building. At Organic, first and second grades shared a room; third and fourth grades shared a room, fifth and sixth grades shared a room, and seventh and eighth grades shared a room. Classes were held in different buildings. Students of all ages in Organic moved around the ten-acre campus to different classes, and sometimes even sat outside under the trees for lessons. Here, teachers led gently, often deferring to us. Our questions ranked foremost on the academic agenda. I wasn't sure I could handle the freedom.

First off, what did "Bell Building" mean? I was certain it was named for a Mr. or Mrs. Bell, some formidable, forbidding bureaucrat not unlike those in that red-brick school.

The first day of school I discovered that the Bell Building *was* the building with the bell in it. Dr. Campbell, the principal, pointed it out to us. "See that white building where the children are sitting in the windows?"

I was not only in fourth grade, as I would have been in the old brick prison in Mobile, I was in "Second Life," the Organic School term for those two grades, third and fourth, that shared a room. Best of all, I was in Mabel Gender's class. Mrs. Gender was one of the older, wiser teachers, who had studied Teachers' Training under Marietta Johnson, the school's founder and a pioneer in child-centered education. Although she had died in 1938, Mrs. Johnson's school still functioned much as it had in her lifetime. Its theory is still in the vanguard of educational thinking.

In 1949, it wasn't easy being the new kid, but it was not unpleasant, either. Mrs. Gender was a strong and loving teacher. Children always want to love their teachers, but so often the public school system denies this basic relationship in the impersonal transactions of forms, requirements to be met, behavior to be corrected. Mrs. Gender, in addition to teaching us the basic lessons for third and fourth grade, read books to us, helped us design sand tables with objects that illustrated what we were studying, and had us write stories and act in short plays.

Once they got past my shyness (my natural assumption that I was going to get things wrong and probably be lost and forgotten somewhere), the other Second Lifers became family to me. Several are still in my life, providing deep friendships that have survived the years. I was comfortable among them, a group of generous, happy children who faced the world with wonder instead of fear. School was something it had never been for me. It was a challenge as well as a delight.

Our teachers were accessible and interested in us as people. John Campbell, the principal I mentioned earlier, was an almost-elfin, lovable little man. We greeted him happily when we passed, as we changed classes during the changing seasons, walking between buildings like big people. We moved to the tile Arts and Crafts Building for pottery, weaving, and shop and to the big community hall on the campus for our daily class in folk dancing. The bell in the Bell Building heralded class breaks with a comforting ring.

A new girlfriend told me that Dr. Campbell could stand on his head. What a thing to say about the school principal! One day, we passed Dr. Campbell on the campus, and my friend stopped him.

"Dr. Campbell, would you stand on your head? Mary Lois is new, and she doesn't believe you can!"

The group he was with laughed. "Stand on my head? Well, all right," he said. He put a large book he was carrying on the ground and proceeded to stand on his head on it. My friend Judy and I jumped for joy, and everybody around applauded. From then on, whenever I passed Dr. Campbell I begged him to stand on his head—and he always did. His wife, the lovely white-haired lady who taught high school history and mathematics, would smile benignly and say, "John really shouldn't be doing that at his age."

There were always a Christmas Pageant and a Spring Festival, both involving the whole school. The school made an effort to democratize events—they were not designed to showcase any particular student's talent or beauty, but to give each child a chance to perform for an audience and to share in the collaborative art that is theatre.

The first year, *Hansel and Gretel* was the production, with the beautiful Humperdinck music and parts for younger children. Most in Second Life (including me) were gingerbread men, with no speaking parts, but everyone in the school was in the pageant. It was an unforgettable experience. I grew up with a deep interest in the theatre, becoming a professional actress, director, and producer of plays. I have little doubt that the school pageants contributed to this life choice.

Spring Festivals were a schoolwide celebration, beginning with folk dancing on the campus. New students were gradually absorbed into the well-oiled dance machine, evolving from awkward, unhappy dancers to smooth participants in the cultural exchange and physical challenge that is folk dance. And you could see them learning to enjoy the process. The same thing happened as they became comfortable with pottery, weaving, and art.

The Festival featured displays of student handiwork in the Arts and Crafts Building and, after the afternoon dances, a huge picnic spread with baked ham and potato salad. More folk dancing, singing, and often a play followed in the evening.

The whole school, arranged in the democratic, "Organic" way by height, beginning with the shortest students and ending with the tallest, began the Festival by dancing the "Processional." The dancers filed onto the green, girls in flowered jumpers with white full-sleeved blouses, boys in white pants and white shirts. The "Recessional," the last dance of the afternoon, involved the whole school, ending with tots stumbling determinedly as they waved big white handkerchiefs one way and then the other. As always at Organic events, the little kids admired the older ones, watching them perform the more beautiful, advanced dances.

There was a lovely high school girl, with a ready smile and an admirable spirit. She was a cheerleader, and involved in all activities. including folk dances, even though she had one arm cut off just below the elbow. She was so well-adjusted and happy that one never noticed or thought of it as a handicap until the moment in folk dancing in which a circle held hands and the audience saw that someone would have to hold that amputated arm. It always went smoothly. She was a good dancer, and that was all that mattered.

After my introduction to Organic in Mrs. Gender's class, I moved to a new "Life Group," Third Life, in which my fifth-grade class was paired with sixth-graders. We were taught by a strange lady whose name was Mary Washington Offut. Miss Offut was almost a total embarrassment; something about her seemed crazy, even to us. She would sit on the campus cross-legged and open her mouth to the sun; she told us this was good for the tonsils. She taught us to do this, and even suggested we roll our opened eyes to sunbathe our eyeballs, but Mrs. Horne, science teacher and concerned parent, intervened, taking some of us aside to inform us this should be avoided as it was not safe.

Miss Offut made me even more self-conscious by teaching us a form of modern dance based on what she considered Greek dancing. We were to swing like elephants, that is, as elephants sway their trunks, and swoop our arms toward the sun, that sort of thing. We gave demonstrations of this art to the high school students, who tried very hard not to laugh at us, but I for one still felt a laughingstock.

When I think about it, however, I remember learning much in Miss Offut's classes. During the day we read the Greek myths surrounding the stars and pasted gold stars onto blue paper representing the constellations, and at night we met on the campus to find the actual constellations in the skies. Nothing was more exciting than the class meeting on the campus on cool nights, gathering on a knoll outside our classroom and searching the heavens for stars we'd pasted into configurations on our paper—the belt and sword of Orion, the hunter; the tiny cluster of the "seven little sisters," the Pleiades, in the center of the winter sky; the two bears, Ursa Minor and Ursa Major, whose dipper shapes pointed out the North Star.

In a study of China, Miss Offut showed us Chinese calligraphy. I'll never forget the moment she showed us how to produce the character that represented "tree." Each stroke required to produce it represented a tonal sound. The character was a pictograph; it actually looked something like a tree. "Forest" combined several tree-symbols. I realized in that moment the essence of language—and the reality that all languages are not necessarily like English, read from left to right, in construction literal and cerebral. Language reflects the culture from which it comes. And what do you know, they are not just like us! This may seem like a large concept for a ten-year-old, but I remember the moment I was struck by it, like a thunderbolt, in a class taught by a creative if controversial teacher.

Field trips to people at work in unusual occupations were a hallmark of the concept of Organic Education. Miss Offut took our class to visit the blacksmith, whose shop was in a shack across Fairhope Avenue from the campus, where there is now a little park with picnic tables. The blacksmith was burly, of course, and covered with soot and grime from his ironwork. During the visit he showed us how he made horseshoes, complete with flying sparks and ringing anvil, and we recited Longfellow's "The Village Blacksmith" for him and sang Handel's "The Harmonious Blacksmith"—"Oh, the blacksmith's a fine, sturdy fel-low..." I wondered even then what the blacksmith thought of *us* that day, as we peered across at him doing his daily tasks.

And even with my memories of humiliation at dancing in the techniques Miss Offut taught, today I look at pictures of my class in the Organic yearbook of 1952 and see some joyous faces, including mine, of little girls dancing and playing in their modern dance costumes—certainly looking for all the world as if they were happy and free.

I cannot write about the Organic School without describing what has often seemed to me to be the happiest year of my life: My first year in Junior High. Clara Campbell was our teacher, and we had two exuberant room mothers who planned recreation for us: a party every single Friday night, in our schoolroom. Junior High Recreation was a tradition at Organic, or I think it was. All I know is that it was a time of enormous fun and social growth for me.

For Junior High Recreation, we played old-fashioned games like "Heavy, Heavy Hangs Over Your Head" which required performances, and Musical Chairs, which required agility and a spirit of fun. I couldn't imagine any place I'd rather be than our room in the Bell Building on Friday nights. In the spring the room mothers, the ever-young Helene Hunter and the fun-loving eccentric Virginia Austin, staged a scavenger hunt of rare objects distributed all over Fairhope—in the gullies, in town, under bushes, down by the beach. It was an extravaganza of literary clues and local lore, filling a Saturday with exploration. At the end of the day, of course there was a class picnic.

The campus had much open space. Here and there were oaks and azaleas, with the heavy old wisteria vine, big enough for climbing, often populated by younger students, just outside Recreation Hall window. The setting was natural and beautiful in its way, but the buildings that covered it were shabby. Most were little cottages that had been moved to the grounds from other places. There was an air of poverty about the place, and it was always a little discomfiting to me to show it to people from other places. Now I recall this atmosphere as part of its uniqueness and that it was *my* need for conformity that made me a little ashamed.

The campus today houses a community college, and the Organic School has moved to smaller quarters across town. When I walk about the community college today, with its lawn manicured and crisp, I look for old shrubs or trees I might recognize, a rusty water fountain, or a familiar ramshackle building. Not that I expect to find them, but the heart holds its memories, and however the campus may be beautified, I seek its past.

It took me years to discover that in the world outside Organic, there is something suspect about having *loved* the school you attended. It was too hard to explain to people who had spent their lives nursing an active dislike of school. This conflict often creates in the Organic graduate an unnecessary defensiveness, as if we were the ones who are wrong. The world is full of people who want to do something about the educational system; unfortunately, these reformers seldom want to hear of a school that works as well as ours.

After returning to my hometown, I sat on a panel of Organic graduates discussing our school. When it came my turn to talk, I described what I remembered, and said something that occurred to me as I listened to the common experiences of the school that I shared with these graduates. I said, "One thing that comes back to me is the memory that we spent the summers and Christmas breaks anticipating when school would open. *We would rather be in school than on vacation.*"

There were always friends who transferred away to other schools for various reasons, such as the boys who defected so that they could play football, or people whose parents had sent them to Organic temporarily and put them back in the public school system when they had gained the confidence or skills to compete in a traditional school. Often the latter students were to regret the move back all their lives. We missed them, but it didn't matter much. The Organic School lacked glamorous events where students were voted "prettiest" and "most popular" and dressed up in evening gowns to receive awards, yet we knew that our bond to our school was what counted. Competition based on one's natural gifts seemed unfair at best. It was not the Organic way.

Although we wouldn't have said it at the time, we felt there was something sacred about our school. In my graduating class, some had parents who were graduates of Organic; others, families who had moved to Fairhope generations before because of the school. We cherished anecdotes about Marietta Johnson, whose pictures hung here and there, and whose name was often invoked as teachers sought to practice her methods.

We knew that education itself and our attitude toward it would be crucial to us throughout our lives. This lesson, so hard to grasp in a traditional setting, had been basic to us since earliest childhood: True education is organic, part of the human condition, and its measure is not taken by test scores. Its measure is taken by the life we live.

Fairhope People

Marietta Johnson, 1938

Marietta Johnson

O F ALL THE UNREALISTIC, DREAM-DRIVEN NONCONFORMISTS ever to call Fairhope home, the most remarkable was Marietta Johnson. Her educational work continues today and influences the more trendy child-centered private schools in major population centers.

In the early days of the twentieth century, Mrs. Johnson's revolutionary views were to reverberate from Fairhope through the educational systems across the world. From 1907 until her death in 1938, she devoted her enormous energies to a laboratory school in the firm belief that the world was ready to replace outmoded educational institutions with those based on new discoveries about childhood and the development of the child.

Mrs. Johnson came to Fairhope with her family in the late 1890s. The choice was natural for her, her husband, and infant son, as she and her husband, ardent Single-Taxers, found a comfort and challenge within the Utopian vision. Even with a number of luminaries—including Upton Sinclair and Clarence Darrow—visiting Fairhope for brief periods of time, Marietta Johnson would become one of the few citizens of Fairhope to achieve world prominence.

Her arrival in Fairhope seemed to produce a perfect fit of person to place. She had been a teacher all her life, but at the age of 38 she became disillusioned with teaching in traditional ways. Like many in Fairhope, she was a visionary. She was obsessed with education. She envisioned education improved in a way that she assumed would be as obvious to the world as it was to her.

Mrs. Johnson reinvented herself once she moved to Fairhope permanently—and she was in her forties at that time. She became a spellbinding lecturer, an accomplished fund-raiser, and a spokesperson for the Progressive Education movement. She was one of the founders of the Progressive Education Association.

By turns charming and confrontational, Marietta Johnson was at home among both the wealthy and the underprivileged. Once she identified her mission to save children from the tyranny of a flawed system, she was indefatigable and relentless in her zeal to set things right. However, up until that epiphany (which occurred in Fairhope), she was simply an excellent teacher, not unlike many women working in the days when school teac hing was almost the *only* acceptable career path for them. She wrote, "I enjoyed a measure of success and used to pity those who had never taught school. It was the most thrilling work I could imagine."

She had worked not only as a teacher but as what was called a "critic" of teachers in the normal schools in her home state of Minnesota. She took pride in the achievements of her students, who, in the traditional way, could read well, memorize, and pass tests with good grades.

In Minnesota, she began to learn of books on the development of the child, and the nature of real learning. These books explained new theories about children—the beginning of studies on child development and natural learning patterns. Her supervisor presented her with a copy of a book called *The Development of the Child*, published by Nathan Oppenheim in 1898, with the admonition, "Unless education shifts its course to conform with these discoveries, it cannot expect to hold the attention of the best of you young teachers."

Upon reading this work, Mrs. Johnson despaired that her life's work up until that point had been a waste, and possibly even destructive to children. The book brought about something of an epiphany for her. Having read it, she went back to this administrator and told him, "The scales are off. If I ever have a child of my own, he will not be put at books until he is at least ten years of age."

The scales are off. What a vivid way to say it! In later interviews she was to say of this first book of many she would read on child development, "It was a real scale-dropper." The remarkable thing about the way the lady comes off the page is how amusing and contemporary she sounds.

Married to a gentle Swede who enjoyed farming and agreed with her views on the theory of Single Tax, Marietta Johnson had made several visits from Minnesota to Fairhope around the turn of the century. The first visit was for Christmas, and the story of their arrival has the Johnsons leaving St. Paul in a snowstorm and arriving in Fairhope to find flowers in bloom and the air like a Minnesota summer. They were immediately smitten with the place.

Having ostensibly given up teaching, Mrs. Johnson nonetheless agreed to teach at Fairhope's first public school. She had immediately connected with the intellectual tenor of the little settlement, and was fast making friends with whom she endlessly discussed her theories about children and the nature of education.

The Johnsons had moved to the South for their health and planned to get back into farming. Difficult as it is to reconcile with the life Marietta Johnson was soon to experience, the Johnsons actually left Fairhope for a time to buy and work a pecan farm in Mississippi. This period must have been a considerable strain on Marietta, as she was torn between her responsibility as a wife and mother and her zeal to create a school system that would transform all of mankind.

However, she committed herself to her duties as a farm wife, at the same time reading as much social criticism and educational theory as she could find time for. She was inspired by Jean-Jacques Rousseau, the great figure of the French Enlightenment who propounded the theory of man as "noble savage"; Friedrich Froebel, who fathered the concept of kindergarten; Nathan Oppenheim, the pediatrician at New York's Mt. Sinai Hospital who had written the work on child development that launched Mrs. Johnson's journey into progressive education; C. Hanford Henderson, then headmaster of the Pratt Institute in New York City; and John Dewey, America's preeminent educational philosopher. Though in reality working hard as a farm wife and mother of a toddler and an infant, she still dreamed of having her own school where she could put her principles into practice. From the Mississippi farm, she kept in contact with her Fairhope friends, who found her devotion to her educational theories an inspiration.

When the pecan farm failed, one of the friends from Fairhope offered her a stipend of $25 a month to run her dream school. It was all the incentive she needed. At this point she and her husband and two little boys moved to Fairhope for good.

It was an exciting time to be alive, particularly if you were an idealist, and even more particularly if you were an idealist living in Fairhope. The citizens of Fairhope—about 200 at this time, drawn to radical theories about almost everything—were extremely encouraging to the bright-eyed little lady with the revolutionary ideas about education. Her friend E. B. Gaston, founder of the town, editor of its weekly newspaper, and father of five, was an avid supporter of her and her school from the first. She and he agreed on Single Tax theory, and he saw in her another opportunity to promote Fairhope on the world stage through his newspaper.

Mrs. Johnson was undoubtedly a delightful person. She had an informal, modern way about her as she spoke extemporaneously and expounded, explained, cajoled, and inspired people with her descriptions of her school. Once she established her school as a laboratory to prove her ideas, there was simply no holding her back. Her husband now assumed a supporting role in her saga—he taught manual training in her school and appears to have been exceedingly proud of her late-found success.

Marietta Johnson's idea of education was as simple as it was radical. The word "education," she believed, was synonymous with life itself; that *as long as one lives one is being educated.* She knew that children learn as they play, and she felt play was one of the most important ways a child could learn. She felt that the most constructive thing a teacher could do was provide the tools to help a child learn what he wanted to learn. *Her school did not grade its children, or have periodic tests and examinations.* The learning was up to the child; she steadfastly maintained that no test score or grading system proved anything.

Her school was radical. There were no dress codes. Music, folk dancing, and arts and crafts were required—and liberal use was made of Fairhope's natural resources in the education of the students. Children acted out the Greek myths as they took hikes to the gullies. They built boats and took apart automobiles. They sat outdoors to do their lessons. They came to school barefooted and spent recess climbing trees. In a word, they were *happy* at their school. This was a school that, in its heyday in the early 1920s, was the center of activity of the little town and a magnet for people who wanted an unconventional educational experience for their offspring.

This idea behind her school inspired other educators. Educational philosophers like John Dewey advocated similar theories. Mrs. Johnson had the respect of such thinkers because, although many *wrote* of the viability of the idea, she actually put a plan to prove it into action by creating an experimental school. And she devoted her life to finding ways to keep this school going.

In 1913 Marietta Johnson was to have a major breakthrough for her experimental school. The philosophical giant John Dewey, an innovator in the area of education, planned a visit to critique her work. Dewey had met Mrs. Johnson through members of The Fairhope League, a fund-raising women's auxiliary sponsoring Mrs. Johnson's Edgewood School in Connecticut. At the time, Dewey was researching a book about the schools around the country that were trying out progressive education.

Mr. Dewey, an extremely respected (and busy) man, was able to set aside a few days to travel to Fairhope, but the only days he could spare were in late December 1913, when the school would be closed for Christmas recess. Mrs. Johnson called a meeting of her pupils and asked them if they would mind continuing classes so that Mr. Dewey could observe them at school, and they voted unanimously to do so. All of Fairhope was excited to have John Dewey visit.

Mrs. Johnson wrote that "the thought of being investigated together with the fear that his report might be unfavorable constituted the most critical experience of my life!"

Indeed, the fate of her school probably did hang upon Dr. Dewey's words. What a relief and joy it must have been to her, then, to have received word of his note to the secretary of the Fairhope League: "...I was pleased even beyond my expectations with what I saw at the Organic School." Dewey was to publish several articles praising Mrs. Johnson's work in Fairhope, and when his book *Schools of Tomorrow* was printed in 1915, he devoted a chapter to her school and what he had seen there. He had brought along his son on his visit to the school, and the youngster begged to be allowed to stay in Fairhope as a student at Organic. The boy said to his father, "All the children are crazy about the school!"

Dewey's praise was unlimited. The elder statesman of American philosophy and education had given a ringing endorsement to Marietta Johnson's work. As a result attention was drawn from all over the world to Fairhope. The school had the imprimatur of an unassailable expert, and it was on its way to a grand period of success.

The publicity the school gained from the publication of *Schools of Tomorrow* in 1915 was enormous. Teachers wanted to learn from Mrs. Johnson; artists wanted to be on the staff of her school; socialites wanted her to give lectures and coach them on child rearing afterwards; philanthropists were interested in sponsoring her school, and both her school and Fairhope reaped the rewards. The 1920s were a peak of intellectual life in Fairhope, largely due to the interest generated by the school.

Mrs. Johnson had long been traveling in rarefied air. The days of exhausting train travel combined with the heady excitement of meeting the likes of Mrs. Alexander Graham Bell (who sponsored her in a series of lectures), Hon. and Mrs. William Howard Taft, Mrs. Woodrow Wilson, Mr. and Mrs. Henry Ford, and other wealthy notables, must have been as stressful as it was exhilarating. Her health and that of her husband had not been good even before the transformation of their lives from schoolteacher and farmer to illustrious educator and her spouse. The new challenges were to take their toll.

Her school is probably the oldest continuously operating progressive school in the world. In all its years there had been a sense of impending trauma in anticipation that in the next school year funds would not be sufficient for its operation. In her day, the school was a magnet to dynamic, interesting teachers, and there were always a number of them who were willing to work for abysmally low pay for the opportunity of teaching in her unusual school. These extraordinary teachers, working with Marietta Johnson, created a climate of creative intellect in Fairhope that was to last for years.

The Great Depression was a painful time for Mrs. Johnson and her school. The interest in progressive education waned, and the association she had founded in the previous decade no longer considered her work crucial. Her health was failing as she entered her seventies, yet she toiled vigorously to prove that her theory of education was not a fad but a valid approach upon which the future depended. She was no longer able, however, to tolerate the lecture schedules she had in the past, and she suffered a serious heart condition and a few small strokes that kept her all but bedridden the last year of her life. Living on the school campus, she still taught the occasional class, and made a speech to the locals when she felt the urge.

She died in December 1938. Grief all but engulfed Fairhope. This wave of disbelief and sorrow reached around the world to her many friends and former students. The sense of great loss penetrated even to children, who knew only that Marietta Johnson had been the center of their little town and their parents' hope for their future.

The teachers at the school banded together to ensure its continuation for the first years after Mrs. Johnson's death. Ultimately, it was the very town of Fairhope—many of those who had been educated by her and now wanted to provide a similar education for their children—who came forth every year to see that the school would continue to provide Organic Education in Fairhope. Sixty-three years later the School of Organic Education school is still operating, still attempting to adhere to the principles she so firmly believed in.

Marietta Johnson's revolution in education is far from over; her work is reflected in the growth of many private schools across the country—Waldorf, Montessori, many Country Day and other alternative schools—the list is long. The leaders of these schools probably don't know it, but all owe a debt to the doughty little teacher from St. Paul who came to Alabama a century ago to change her life and change the world.

Today a statue of Marietta Johnson sits on Fairhope's bluff, placed by the Marietta Johnson Museum, which now occupies the Bell Building of what was once the School of Organic Education. The statue depicts Mrs. Johnson flanked by figures of children with books and bare feet, in rapt attention to their teacher. The work was inspired by the photo taken by John Dewey in 1913 for his book *Schools of Tomorrow*. It places Mrs. Johnson doing what she did best in one of her favorite places on the planet.

Her school has never closed its doors. Its director and board of managers are committed to Mrs. Johnson's work of educating the next generation with a process as natural as breathing, proving almost a hundred years later that education is simply life.

Winifred Duncan

Winifred Duncan

"Miss Claverly—did I mention her?—oh, yes. She is
that strange insect woman who lives on the edge of
the gully. You can't have met her yet, but you will, for
she is hard to miss. She is strange, strange, with her
nets and queer talk. When she walks uptown, traffic
practically stops, dogs howl, and babies cry. For, oh
dear, I really can't do her justice. She can't be described. She lives all alone with four bloodhounds and
does all sorts of weird things. We tried to get her to
come to our little teas, but after one appearance it was
enough for us and, I'm afraid, for her."

Robert E. Bell
The Butterfly Tree

MORE THAN ONCE Winifred Duncan was picked up by the
Fairhope police in the middle of the night for canoeing in
the nude. A lifelong iconoclast and twitter of conformists,
on these occasions she displayed only contempt for the police, since,
as she said, she was harming no one.

Miss Duncan was bizarre in appearance, with stick-straight,
colorless hair (it might have once been red) cut in a Buster Brown bob

almost to her shoulders. She often wore men's suits. She had been a dancer—it was said, with the troupe of Isadora Duncan—before she took to investigating the insects and microscopic life about her. She had also been a sculptor of some repute and, as the poems she wrote indicate, a writer as well.

Her interest in insects led her to an intense study of them, which she chronicled in a most successful book called *Webs in the Wind*. The book featured Winifred Duncan's elegant drawings and information about spiders. Late in her life she was often referred to as "the spider lady," but I never heard her called that. She was Winifred, or Miss Duncan. We were in awe of her, and we realized that there was something very special there.

Miss Duncan was intimidating, particularly to us children, I suppose perhaps because there was something decidedly witch-like about her appearance. I wish I had been old enough, as Bob Bell had been, to appreciate—even enjoy—that tinge of madness she wore like a badge. Bob and his friend Andrew Dacovich became very attached to her. Bob's correspondence to me describes the two of them sitting amongst her almost-enchanted cats and listening to her offbeat pronouncements.

She was a principal character, the scientist "Miss Claverly," in his novel *The Butterfly Tree*. As far as I know the bloodhounds in the excerpt above were pure fiction. Bob's perception of her attracting attention in Fairhope also strikes me as a false note. Growing up with her in the picture, I do not recall her eccentricities causing much of a stir. She was interesting, amusing, and even exasperating, but hardly the stopper of traffic he describes. In recalling his friendship with her years later Bob wrote:

> I hardly know where to begin with Winifred. Andrew Dacovich dropped by one sizzling afternoon just before I left for Harvard and wanted to take me to meet "a very interesting person." Winifred had just moved to Fairhope and lived in a

little cottage in an alley between Kiefer and Powell Streets that started just across the street from my house. I was immediately fascinated with her, particularly when I found she had lived in Cambridge for a couple of years. I think I saw her another couple of times before I left that fall. When I came home for Christmas she had moved, I think, to the house she bought over the gully from North Church Street. When I came home from Harvard I, she, and Dac were a veritable triumvirate. We went everywhere together. She had a dozen interests, and I could find her in the afternoons choreographing cat ballets or looking into microscopes at scum she had collected from ponds. I think both her books, *Webs in the Wind* and *The Private Life of the Protozoa*, were in print by that time. She prevailed upon me to join her in doing the tango, and she walked me through some intricate maneuvers. I could only imagine what we must have looked like had anyone seen us moving about the room on one of those evenings. She had her cats—all three named Mimi, so she would have to call them only once. Dinner at her house was an adventure, since the cats were not discouraged from joining us at the table—*on* the table, I mean. She introduced me to her favorite books and authors, and she was interested in mine. She had a succession of strange people living with her for short periods of time. There was a very talkative woman whose conversation revolved around her children and grandchildren...then came Gertrude Norman, a really weird woman who kept to her room. I would be there and suddenly a long white arm would appear through a crack in the door and pick up the phone and take it into her room, where she would order gin...Then came Michael Finley, whom Winifred had known in an earlier life. He was a rather saturnine young man, darkly handsome, who dressed every afternoon, no matter how hot, in a black pinstriped suit and sat eating licorice candies from a jar on the table. He drank a lot, and he and Winifred quarreled.

Winifred was into metaphysical things. When I first met her she was doing theosophy. She and I attended the Unitarian church one Sunday. I dropped by one evening, and she met me at the door: "Darling, you can't come in right now. We are having a séance." This last was one of the very first dianetics groups.

Once Dac, Michael, Winifred and I drove to Pensacola Beach, which at that time was still an old-fashioned beach with a large casino.* We sunned first, and Winifred had forgotten to put on the top of her bathing suit. She proceeded to bare her upper body and put on the top with total nonchalance, although we were surrounded by hundreds of people. Later we walked into the casino, which had a large dance floor. As we stood there watching a few people dance, Winifred suddenly put her hands above her head and slowly turned across the floor to the opposite side. The dancing couples left the space to her, and she was twirling all alone on the big dance area. Just one of the many things I remember.

Dr. Dacovich recalled an evening when he and Bob went to supper with Winifred and she served the Greek wine retsina. Aged in pine, retsina takes on an astringent taste, reminiscent of the pine resin it's named after. The three drank and drank, and Dacovich swore that as he and Bob walked home late that night, squirrels followed them all the way. He and Bob couldn't stop laughing at the entourage. They were convinced they were so saturated with retsina that they smelled like pine trees, and that was attracting the squirrels.

To say that the multifaceted Winifred Duncan was strange is like acknowledging that Van Gogh was a little different from other painters. But she brought to her unusualness a word that Bob used earlier—nonchalance. Miss Duncan was nonchalant about her strangeness, comfortable in her unconventional looks. She seemed to be unaware that her *life* was anything unusual.

I recall her attending a the Fairhope Little Theatre performance, and seeing her rise from her front-row seat in the middle of the first

---

Casino was the word used on the Gulf Coast in the early twentieth century to describe a public bathhouse, principally for changing clothes.

scene to announce, "I understand there's a good movie on," as she stalked out of the building.

I have heard horror stories about her table manners, as in the time when, taken to luncheon at the Grand Hotel, shoveling the food into her face like a starving refugee, she proceeded to talk with her mouth full, spraying her companions, generally embarrassing her hostess, who had perceived her as interesting rather than uncouth. She was herself, wherever she was. It was not always pleasant, but it was no act.

The Fairhope Library houses a room for Fairhope literature, and somewhere in it is a handmade scrapbook in which Miss Duncan had typed up some poetry as a gift to Anna Braune. Most had been published in New York newspapers, from the days when New York newspapers printed poetry. In chronicling her relationship to the nature of her life, these poems present a new picture of the woman. They also withstand the tests that set apart beautiful, unpretentious writing.

On Mobile Bay

Over the wide-lipped kiss of wave on sand
The sea-winds hover.
Fretting and stroking the smooth water-skin
Like a shy lover.
Carving designs there that sing
Like a butterfly's wing.

Wave does not care for wind's loving; slips out from under,
Shimmering with passion;
Flings at the cold, hard sand, sucks at it,
Trying to fashion
Hollows, where she can rest, in the sand's breast.

Sand, weary of the endless kiss of the sea,
Creeps, grain by grain,
Sly but determined, up through the seaweed and wrack,
Trying to gain
The warm lap of earth; wanting to know
The velvet-soft push of
Things that grow.

(Published by the *New York Tribune*)

Fairhope Pet Cat

When I was a panther bold, dear,
And you were a bumble bee,
And buzzed at my ear in jungles deep,
Spoiling my beautiful noonday sleep,
I'm sure the forest shook to see
How bold you were at teasing me.

Now it is I who hover near,
So humbled by your haughty face
I do not dare to buzz into
Your charming, furry ear.

Which sadly demonstrates, you see,
What evolution's done to me
Since I was a panther bold, dear,
And you were a bumble bee.

(Published by *Poetry Magazine*)

Fairhope Pet Cat No. 2
(Three years later)

You need not look at me like that,
And wave your tail, and softly knead
My busy knee, with your front feet;
I know that all it means is meat.

You need not push your velvet head,
Nor make those purring sounds, like silk.
I am aware that all this charm
Means only that you want your milk.

But when, at dawn, rain soaked, you come,
And push against the windowpane,
And yelp, and show your bitten ear,
And wet the bed—ah, then—
I know I have not loved in vain!

In later life, Miss Duncan became disoriented and had to be encouraged to stay at what was then known as Mrs. Beasley's Rest Home. It was not in her character to tolerate such an institution, no matter how ill she could manage on her own. She became increasingly hostile and paranoid, and insisted that things were being stolen from her, she was being mistreated, she wouldn't stand for this, etc. Mrs. Beasley herself was as patient as anyone could have been with her, but Miss Duncan would have none of it, and ultimately packed her bags to leave Fairhope for good.

She was last seen boarding a Greyhound bus with all her belongings, telling her alarmed acquaintances that she was moving to Mexico for a new life.

Miss Duncan could not have known her effect upon Fairhope during her life there and the curiosity she would arouse as a symbol of its years as a haven for unique people. Such a rich and intriguing life she led—with her stubbornness, her good old nonchalance, and her commitment to a life in which she answered to her own heart.

"Prof" Oliver Mark Taylor, 1962

"Prof"

H E WAS TALL AND GANGLY, intellectual looking with his dark-rimmed spectacles and outsized Adam's apple. Poor as a church mouse and Bohemian without trying. The absent-minded professor with a difference, he was quite unlike anyone our young eyes had ever seen. We didn't know much about him, really, except that he was our teacher, and he *belonged* at the Organic School in Fairhope, Alabama.

When Oliver Mark Taylor had first come to Fairhope from Baltimore in the mid-1930s, he had been a serious young man, a first-rate scholar probably lured to town through contacts in the Northeast. He was a friend of Jim Preu, who came to teach at the school. Possibly he heard Marietta Johnson lecturing about her educational theory and came to Fairhope to learn from her. His special interests were English and the theatre, which he would teach along with history, journalism, and other courses at the Organic School. He is remembered in Fairhope from his first stay here in the 1930s as an excellent teacher, the kind who could open your mind and inspire you to work on your own. In that period he directed the Organic high school youngsters in such plays as *The School for Scandal*, and he helped students put together their first official newspaper, *The Organic Merry-Go-Round.*

He later told us how they had agonized looking for a name for the publication, and at last chose to lift the name from Drew Pearson's popular syndicated column "The Washington Merry-Go-Round."

On his second stay, in the 1950s, the town viewed him as an odd bird. Prof had a strange way of walking. He had a strange way of talking. To outsiders, he simply seemed strange, but his students looked right past that and listened to what he said. We were aware that as an economy he rolled his own cigarettes, or perhaps he did this to limit his smokes per day. If that was so, however, it didn't work: His fingers were yellow with nicotine stains right up to the first knuckle.

A neurological disorder caused his awkwardness, according to the grownups. But it looked comic to us. He had long legs, and he loped. He lurched. He certainly never thought about how he looked, leaning forward as if into a strong wind and taking great strides without looking where he was going. His balance was uncertain, and his movements could be wildly uncoordinated.

His clear, radio-announcer accent sometimes sounded vaguely English. He punctuated his sentences with phrases like "M'deah." Sometimes he would mutter. Sometimes he would bark. He liked to talk out of one side of his mouth, like a gangster in a B-movie. He had a staccato laugh that was frequent—almost a chortle, but it was a smile-less laugh; it would just erupt from him.

He didn't spend time in contemplation. He appreciated a good mind, a bright remark, and a worthwhile kid. He did not have much patience with others. Something about him suggested that he was not sure there was enough time to do what he was going to do. This abruptness may have simply been because he was not Southern. He operated on a different clock from many in Fairhope. He always seemed to be on his way somewhere.

There was some excitement when he returned to teach at Organic in the 1950s. We heard was there was to be a new male teacher in the high school, that he wasn't married, and that he was our parents' age.

He appeared at Clean-Up Day that fall—the weekend before school started, when parents, teachers, and students gathered on the campus to spruce up the whole ten acres for upcoming classes.

On Clean-Up Day he worked alongside some high school kids, who liked him right away. They had fallen naturally into calling him "Ollie." My first memory of the man was his correcting the group for this, saying, "I personally don't mind—but the thinking is, if you start calling people by their first names automatically, it doesn't indicate respect. One day you're going to call the boss 'George,' and he won't like it." So we reluctantly called him "Mr. Taylor" for a time.

All his students seemed to need a name more accessible than "Mr. Taylor"—and there *was* that *other* Mr. Taylor, the director of the school, Fletcher M. Taylor. The street-smart high school student Von Gammon came up with "Prof" as a nickname. The grownups called him Ollie, and some called him by his middle name, Mark, which he preferred, but the name that was used for him by a generation was "Prof."

He had a very salty vocabulary, which may have been exacerbated by his World War II experiences. His foul mouth would get him into much trouble in his teaching career, as he simply didn't seem to be able to control it. I'd say he used strong language, yet I never heard him say the F-word (in fact, I don't remember anyone saying that in Fairhope in those days). He certainly had no compunction about damning the whole situation, or asking God to. He just seemed to be making a point. If anything, it got a little old after a time, but his habit did not influence anybody's speech as far as I could tell. I guess enough had heard similar language at home. However, his profanity became a *cause célèbre* for some parents.

He was especially effective teaching adolescents. He treated them as he would treat his peers. He seldom pulled rank. He conducted classes as they would be in college—he came prepared, shared what he knew, and the learning part was up to you. It was his assumption that you were on his level, and this was an automatic challenge to his students.

By the time Oliver Mark Taylor came back to Fairhope to teach in the 1950s he was a qualified psychology teacher, and my class took psychology from him. However, given his wide-ranging interest and knowledge, we often steered the discussion to other topics. We knew he was greatly interested in theatre and movies. He spoke about the stage with an intimate knowledge, as if he were on speaking terms with George S. Kaufmann and Moss Hart, Alexander Woollcott and their friends. When he mentioned H. L. Mencken, he did so with such a familiarity that it seemed he assumed any intelligent person would know whom he was talking about. It was inspiration to run pick up a book and find out just who this Mencken or Woollcott was.

I remember our class challenging him about what constituted a good actor. His response was that good acting is always a matter of opinion. He maintained that if people paid money year after year to see a certain actor, that was evidence enough that the actor was talented. You can imagine the incredulous response this received. Nobody in the class felt that commercial viability was a fair assessment of acting ability.

We said, "How about Kim Novak?"

He had never seen her, but said if she had been a star for over three years, she was a good actress. There happened to be a Kim Novak movie at the Fairhope Theatre that week. We insisted that he go to see it—and we wanted his opinion *after* seeing her work.

At the next class, he announced that Kim Novak was a very good actress.

Catcalls and boos from all seven in the little room.

The movie was *Jeanne Eagles*, and Prof, who didn't feel like paying for a ticket or sitting through the whole show, had entered free for the last twenty minutes or so.

"She was doing a drunk scene," he announced. "She performed the wavering in and out of the stupor—not an easy acting job—very convincingly. She can act." We demurred, but I guess you would say we lost that argument. At any rate, I have been taking his side about the performer whom audiences will pay to see as being a valid criterion for acting ever since.

My older sister Billye had a special rapport with him. An exceptional scholar with a special interest in the subjects he taught, she appreciated his oddness and his treatment of her as an equal. She wanted to be in plays, and he encouraged her to write them herself, which she did. She spent much energy in high school writing plays with glamorous parts for herself, which he would direct. It was an effective collaboration, based upon mutual respect and shared goals—putting on plays. And her plays were good.

Prof was full of theatre stories. He was very original in expressing matters relating to the stage. Once when directing a high school play, he told one boy not to cross his knees onstage because the shoe sole on the dangling foot, seen from the audience, resembled "the moon rising slowly out of an ash heap."

When helping budding playwrights, he opined that in a one-act play "An Indian has got to bite the dust within the first ten minutes."

One of my favorite Prof-isms was about putting on plays for the evening's entertainment at our spring folk-dance and song festival. He said, "Why put on a play as an adjunct to a plate of potato salad?"

Because Billye had written plays, I wanted to write plays too. I wrote a one-act that was to be presented for Spring Festival, regardless of the potato salad. I designed the play for an all-girl cast since there were all girls in my class. It was inspired by my notion at that time that it would be fun to spend the night alone in a department store after all the employees had gone home. My plot involved some girls who got locked in a department store while, at the same time, female robbers had broken in to steal merchandise. I remember having some difficulty working out what would happen from there, but finally I came up with an ending. Under Prof's direction the class worked on the play for weeks to get it ready.

Unfortunately, it wasn't ready the night before the Festival. The dress rehearsal was a shambles. Few knew any of their lines. I was heartsick that I might *never* be able to compete with my sister on equal footing. At least *her* class cooperated when *she* wrote a play!

My mother sat in on the rehearsal. Driving home we talked about the disaster it was going to be. I said I thought I wanted to withdraw the production. It was a hard concept for my sixteen-year-old mind to get around, but I felt in my heart that I wasn't going to have a success.

I made my first grown-up decision. I would not allow the production.

We drove back to Comings Hall to talk it over with Prof.

The fact was, Prof *lived* in Comings Hall. Literally. He was so broke he couldn't afford to live anywhere else. There was a toilet in there, and he had an Army cot in a little anteroom, and it was somehow okay with him. If anything exemplifies what a very different town Fairhope was then, perhaps that situation—the respected teacher living on no money in a corner of one of the school buildings—does. You just don't see it today anywhere—and certainly not in Fairhope.

Back to my theatrical fiasco at Spring Festival, which I must relate because I was so moved by Prof's reaction when he heard my decision. My mother and I turned the car around somewhere about at Seacliff Drive and headed back to Prof in Comings Hall. By the time Mama and I got there he was readying himself for bed.

I told him how upset I was about the way my play looked. I told him I didn't want it to be put on. He simply stood there, hunched over, in his sleeveless T-shirt and his trousers, thought about what I said, and said quietly, "So. The playwright withdraws."

He looked at me through the dark rimmed glasses, raised his eyebrows and went on, "It's been done before."

With assurances that he certainly understood my feeling, and that he would back me up, he sent us on our way. I felt like a different person after that. I was sure that I would appear to be a prima donna for not allowing my play to appear, but now I didn't care. *The playwright withdraws. I was the playwright.*

The next day the news that the play would not be performed buzzed about the school, and I was not reluctant to say why—that it just wasn't ready. I was prepared to take criticism about depriving the audience of a theatrical adjunct to a plate of potato salad. The amazing part was that everyone understood. Even the cast, who claimed to have stayed up the night learning lines, and were very surprised and disappointed not to have their night in the spotlight, could see why I did what I did. I have never been sorry. And I have never forgotten Prof on that night.

There is at least one other event I associate with him. I think it was our senior year that the *other* Mr. Taylor, the school director, decided that the school should mark Pan American Day with a celebration. Our mothers got South American recipes so they might prepare the food; we all were to come in appropriate costumes; Spanish classes would perform skits—and I was Entertainment Chairman. This meant researching South American folk songs and dances and teaching them to the other students.

I remembered the Mexican folk dances we had watched the big kids do under the tutelage of Warren Stetzel years before. The lilting Latin music was beautiful. I found the books of music and instructions and enlisted my classmate Linda Horne as accompanist. She and I worked out the steps from diagrams in the books and rehearsed our pupils over and over, working for absolute accuracy in the dances and harmony in the songs. It took many hours, and I relentlessly pulled people away from other activities, insisting that they work on the program for Pan American Day.

Prof observed all this, shook his head, and said out of one side of his mouth, "Yer a real slave driver!"

I was so proud of that. I was doing what needed to be done. People were accepting my authority. Prof's words had the ring of respect. Ultimately I produced a show of Mexican and South American songs and dances that worked.

In fact, years later when I found myself directing amateur theatre, it felt right because I could remember the process I had learned then. I could almost hear Prof saying what he had said about me at the Pan-American Day rehearsals. It seemed like destiny that the young slave driver would, at age forty, once again push people around a stage to teach them acting—plus coordinate scenery, lights, music, and sound; do publicity; get programs printed; pull together a volunteer box office staff; and sit out front and enjoy the plays. I later took this a step farther by organizing a professional theatre company in Fairhope, always with some memory of Prof as stage director, and the way he worked.

I never had the guts to use the line about the moon rising out of the ash heap. Yet I thought so often of his professional demands and his commitment to what he was doing, often with clueless and uncooperative teenagers, in this little town in the middle of nowhere. Because putting on shows was so much fun for me I tried to make it fun for anybody I worked with in the theatre—amateur and professional—and because of what I learned from Prof I tried to make it meaningful, serious, and grown-up as well.

I only wished he could have been there in the audience. No matter what he might have said, or more likely not said, I know he would have liked it.

Verda Horne

VERDA DOWDLE HORNE was an old-fashioned intellectual. She was a scientist, a writer, a leader, and a teacher. In addition to her specialties of botany, zoology, physics, anthropology, history, and literature, she had an interest in philosophy, poetry, astronomy, the arts, gardening, and being a mother. She subscribed to an unfathomable number of magazines, received even more books in the mail (this was before we had a local bookstore), and read them all. She reviewed books for the magazines. She was the first mother I ever saw actually bake an apple pie from scratch, and, with characteristic speed and expertise, she made it look both easy and fun. Her energy never flagged. Her sentences always parsed. She had an astonishingly large vocabulary.

Verda was a science teacher at the Organic School, and always busy with a million things at once.

About that vocabulary: Somewhere in about the seventh grade I wanted to increase my "word power," a phrase popular at that time. I leafed through the dictionary, picked words that interested me, and attempted to use them as often as I could. Finding a wonderful five-dollar word that meant "never tiring," I began to say "indefatigable" at every opportunity. Mrs. Horne overheard me, and jumped to correct my pronunciation. I was saying in-de-fa-*teeg*-able, assuming that, since the word had to do with fatigue, that was the way to say it. By now it has been incorporated into my vocabulary, but I shall probably always remember her when I say it. Not only did she know how to say it, she exemplified it.

Mrs. Horne was tiny. She might have stood about 5'1" with high heels. She was petite, with a head a little large for her body, and a face a little big for her head. She looked interesting, not pretty but rather handsome if one so diminutive can be called handsome. We didn't think about her that way, as she was all teacher.

She was my friend Linda's mother, and she was certainly not like any of the other mothers. They all seemed to be homebound, creative in their unique ways, yet defined by husband, children, and house. She was a wife and mother, yet played many other roles when that was an unusual thing to do. She was ahead of her time.

Her house had no particular décor. Its rooms were small and literally piled high with books and periodicals. One fall a bird nested in an open window so she couldn't close that window until spring came.

Her husband was landscape architect Rix Horne, a man who moved slowly and thought deliberately. From rural Henry County, at Alabama and Georgia's border, he was an even-tempered, taciturn man. His very aspect projected kindness. Possibly his greatest gift was an ability to appreciate. He was tall and lean, with eyebrows that turned upwards at the arch, almost reversing in the middle. His children Linda and Richard inherited those unique brows.

Verda was like a busy little bird, darting around organizing people, gathering data, working on projects. Most were important. She organized a Unitarian Fellowship in Fairhope and addressed it every week unless there was an important Unitarian in town to whom she would defer the honor.

She was an articulate and intriguing speaker. Supremely confident and thoroughly informed, she provided a wonderful example of what it takes to deliver a talk. She knew what she wanted to say and was able to express herself brilliantly, and it seemed natural for her because she was always knowledgeable about her subject.

What had made her the way she was, and what had brought her to Fairhope? I knew that she was from a Mormon family in Utah, and that they were Danish farm people. She had gone to the University of Minnesota, I presume on a scholarship, and I suppose she had selected it because of a superior department in the sciences. I seem to recall a story that she moved South on some scientific project, and she met her husband while on an expedition to Gulf Shores hunting blue crabs. The pull to be a wife and mother was irresistible, as she was a woman who wanted to achieve and experience all that there could be in life.

She was an excellent no-nonsense cook, concentrating on whole-grain foods, organic vegetables, and some old Danish family recipes. As we entered adolescence she would cook fresh doughnuts for us, particularly for parties I remember at her house where we gathered to watch a summer's meteor showers through a borrowed telescope. There was a summer of star watching in the Hornes' back yard...lying on rugs pulled from here and there in their house, gobbling delicious doughnuts and waiting for stars to fall as we took turns looking through the telescope. Then, at the evening's close, we'd sit in the living room and sing group songs like "Do, Lord" and "In the Evening by the Moonlight." Nobody on earth has ever enjoyed group singing as much as I did.

For some reason, I asked for the recipe for the doughnuts and was told that "Mother never gives out her recipes." The reason was that once long ago she had given a recipe to a friend; the friend served the dish at a party, and when the compliments came, the friend didn't have the courtesy to credit Verda for the recipe. She decided to keep her recipes to herself after that. Maybe she should just have decided to be more careful about her friends. Years later her daughters published a family cookbook, and there among the delightful family stories and cooking lore from all over the country was Verda's recipe for doughnuts.

She was a mentor to many young people. She had an interest in them, but it was mostly an intellectual interest. I felt very comfortable with her, and loved her classes, but I never knew if she appreciated me or not, since my realm was always the lighter things in life—show business and what came to be called "pop culture."

Once in a physical science class, when we were approaching a section on the law of gravity, Mrs. Horne threw out the question, "What was Isaac Newton's contribution to scientific knowledge?"

I took the bait.

"He said, 'What goes up must come down,'" I jumped in quickly.

"No, he didn't. That's the general interpretation of what he said, but it's a distortion," she corrected me.

I realized I was going to learn something. I didn't feel stupid or even any more misinformed than most people, since she had acknowledged that mine was the generally accepted answer. I enjoyed being the one to set her up for a lesson.

"What did he say, then?

"He said, 'Every action...has an equal...and opposite...reaction.'"

I learned something. I have never forgotten it. I have found it to be true in realms that probably even Isaac Newton never imagined.

Verda was an avid bird-watcher and took us on some field trips to count migrating birds. Agony though it was to keep absolutely still for what seemed like hours but was probably just a minute or two, we learned what it takes to study birds—we had to meet them on their terms, hide from them because they were justifiably afraid of us. We learned reverence for those birds, through observation, and we learned to keep scientific records of their travels through our area.

Although I loved her science classes, I performed best work for her when asked to *write* something about science. My mind was not precise, and confronted with her intellectual energy, I always felt a bit lazy. Yet from her I learned what a scientific mind is, how a scientist reasons and the questions a scientists asks after forming a hypothesis. I learned what scientific analysis is.

Her classes were never limited to the topic at hand. In physics class we also learned to produce term papers, to make and keep notes, to annotate footnotes and bibliographies. I produced a paper for biology in which I wanted to use the information from the then-new Surgeon General's Report on Tobacco. The Fairhope library was poorly equipped at that time, so I just used the *Reader's Guide to Periodical Literature* to unearth a few articles about the dangers of smoking and strung them together, blithely paraphrasing, editing, and interpolating. One point I remember was that if you smoke only a few puffs on a king-size, filter cigarette, then discard it, it is less dangerous than smoking right down to the butt where there nicotine and tars are concentrated. It was a pretty good paper. When I presented it in class, Mrs. Horne pondered it for a minute and then asked about the sources.

I told her about my visits to the library and that the articles I found on the subject had come from *Reader's Digest*.

She said, "It's well written—a slick journalistic article. But it wouldn't hold up as a science paper because you got two-thirds of the information from pre-digested material. The research was done by a publication to espouse a particular agenda. Your article ends up saying what the *Reader's Digest* says, that smoking is harmful to your health—but here are ways you can do it without hurting yourself much." She was right. Although it may be a wonderful magazine in some respects, I have never been able to take the *Reader's Digest* seriously since that day.

From teachers like Verda, the lesson was not always specific. I remember her lectures to various groups. She gave a book review of Ann Morrow Lindbergh's *Gifts from the Sea* to the Unitarian fellowship, and then to several other clubs. I heard the talk more than once, and was always touched by her deep and genuine response to the material—and what I got from her talks about the book lasted me all my life. In my mid-fifties, about forty years after her book reviews, I was going through my own self-evaluation in order to make a major decision about my life. I rented a condo at Gulf Shores and went there by myself for a month, with a copy of *Gifts from the Sea* at my side. I reread the book, and thought of Verda, and how much of what I had learned from her transcended the years and transformed my life. How often today I'll think, look out a window, remember a fact, regard a wild bird, and realize again something I learned long ago from Verda Horne.

From her I learned an infinite respect for a reasoning mind, and the importance of thinking a problem through—and I learned just how much there is to know.

From her I learned the scientific vocabulary—*phylum, class,* and *order.*

From her I learned that in increasing my word power, pronunciation was as important as definition. I learned the difference between *Reader's Digest* and *Scientific American.* I even learned the difference between primary and secondary source material.

From her I heard the titles of great books, which would later actually provide the incentive to read some of them.

I was exposed to food made with whole-wheat flour, informing a lifelong interest in cooking healthfully.

I learned to be quiet in the presence of a bird. And I looked through a telescope at the stars.

I did not grow up to be a scientist. Probably without those classes with Mrs. Horne I would never have had the slightest interest in science or its magic. But her enthusiasm and range of knowledge taught me more than the specific disciplines she embraced.

She herself was a challenge: She was a woman living as full a life as she possibly could, with myriad talents to draw upon, a keen intellect, and an inner drive to make things better.

The subtext of her life was that we could learn by observation. We were especially fortunate in having her example to observe.

Verda Horne, 1956

Henry James Stewart, the Hermit of Montrose
1858–1946

The Hermit and the Lady Who Lived in the Trees

O   N THE OUTSKIRTS OF FAIRHOPE, amid a scattering of small
         office buildings, stands a concrete domed structure, a beehive-
         shaped room that was once a man's house. This man lived
alone, grew his own food, and came five miles into town on foot for
occasional meetings and lectures.

On the other side of town, where Section Street came to the edge
of the gully in the old days, there was a house held up by pine trees,
where a lady named Mrs. Schramm lived.

More is known today about Mr. Stuart, the hermit who lived in
the dome, than about Mrs. Schramm, an ordinary citizen of Fairhope
who just happened to live in a tree house. They both deserve mention
in any book about Fairhope, because they both reflect the Fairhope
that once was.

H. J. Stuart was born in Hampshire, England, in 1858.

Apparently he had been reared in Ohio and had worked in
Washington, D.C., as an engineer, yet there is some dispute about his
origins. In an account in her book *Montrose*, Florence Scott places
him in divinity school at Mount Union College in Missouri, and later
in the town of Nampa, Idaho.

He corresponded with Prescott A. Parker, for whom Parker Road in Montrose is named, before deciding to move to South Alabama. Mr. Parker was committed to living on what he could grow himself, and writing about it in little pamphlets called "Keep Close to the Ground."

However Stuart found his way to the South, and, whatever he did prior to his arrival, he made a decidedly new life when he got here. He was clearly disenchanted with modern life. He read widely. Stuart appreciated radical writers and dreamed of living the life Thoreau described in *Walden*. He built his "Tolstoy Park" on ten acres in what was then very secluded land in Montrose.

He built the dome with bricks that were free for the taking from the mouth of Rock Creek, where there had once been brickyards, and from concrete blocks he had made himself. Outside it he had used the extra blocks to create a terrace garden for strawberries and vegetables. He was totally self-sufficient in his park, pumping water from his own well with a windmill and using this pumping system to irrigate his garden.

His little house was filled with books—Tolstoy and Thoreau, of course, but also Walt Whitman's *Leaves of Grass*, Oscar Wilde's *De Profundis*, David Grayson's *Adventures in Contentment* and *The Friendly Road*. He read poetry and the classics, and political works from Tom Paine to Emma Goldman.

Stuart claimed to be an anarchist, but if so he was one in spirit only. He was a handsome old gentleman, with a long white beard and long white hair, chiseled features, and an elegant way of speaking. He never wore shoes or a hat. He lived a life of genuine economy, weaving rugs in his little beehive house, eating the same breakfast every morning, fresh-made mush of equal parts corn and wheat, ground in his own hand mill each day as he needed it. He made this porridge every day by steaming it for two or three hours after breakfast, and ate it the next day. He browned it in the frying pan and poured very sweet tea over it. The remaining tea he sipped with bread or toast. He claimed that this breakfast was ample and cost only three cents.

He shopped in Fairhope, for staples like day-old bread, which he could buy for six cents per loaf rather than ten when fresh. His only tools at home were those used for his garden, a little cooking stove, and a typewriter, at which he was quite adept. He kept up a correspondence with friends from his former life, but in his days in Fairhope he was totally self-sufficient and totally alone.

He wrote a description of a day in his life to a Milford W. Howard, a newspaper columnist for the *Birmingham News-Age-Herald*, in 1929:

On the 9th I went barefooted to Rock Creek and took a dip in that clear, swift water. First plunge was followed by a thorough cleansing with soap, then three more plunges beneath the water before coming out. Delightful? I'll tell the world it was. Again I felt like a boy of 60 years ago at the little brook in Ohio where we used to build a dam for the very purpose of enjoying life in its simplicity far from town or city.

Here at Rock Creek is privacy, even greater than in my home, for the pool in the trail through thick woods is seldom traveled by other than myself as I go for our mail. One margin of the pool is formed by the intertwined roots of a tall pine and gum tree. Other is formed by thick matted vines green all the winter long. A beautiful, tall holly is but a few feet distant and there is sweet bay and maple and oak and poplar close by, forming a delightful shade on the hottest days. Who would give this for anything the city can offer? Not I, I'm sure.

Stuart was not antisocial. When visitors found his dwelling, he proudly showed them around and explained the devices he had designed for his use. He was a friend to Converse Harwell, one of Fairhope's craftsmen and cantankerous early citizens. Harwell was quite taken by Stuart's philosophy, which included this creed, "For orthodox churches I have little use; I worship God in his own temples; I see Him in every bush and every shrub when I walk through the woods."

When he reached his eighties, Stuart's health began to fail, and he left the area "for the West," according to Mrs. Scott. He donated his loom to the Organic School, where it was used for years to come to teach the age-old craft of weaving to generations of youngsters. His odd little beehive house still stands as a curiosity.

Mrs. Schramm, who was a resident of Fairhope, had her house built into a stand of pine trees in the 1920s. The house was about eight feet off the ground, and pines were used as its foundation She was dubbed "The Bird Lady," but it is not known whether she identified with birds or merely wanted the view. She got into her house by way of a ladder, and when she didn't feel like having visitors she pulled the ladder up.

The house was located in what was then the woods at the end of Section Street, near where Pecan intersects with the street today. The only bathtub she had was on the ground below. This fact was known by the children of Fairhope, who found ways through the woods to her house in hopes of spying the lady climbing down from the tree house naked, or at best scantily clad, to take her bath.

Mischievous little boys often taunted her from the ground below, and eventually Mrs. Schramm made a sign which read, "I DON'T LIKE YOUR HOUSE EITHER" and displayed it to discourage the curious.

The hermit and the lady who lived in a tree were long gone before I ever got to Fairhope. Yet occasionally, when I drive on the busy highway as it intersects with Parker Road, I realize that I am near what was once the isolated woodland paradise that H. J. Stuart had made his own. and I contemplate what his life here must have been like.

Or, in the heart of Fairhope, tooling along past the Catholic Church on Section Street, I look to my left at the trees just beyond the houses and wonder just exactly where Mrs. Schramm's home was. I would like to explore both places.

Even though the two have passed into mythology now, I miss them.

Mrs. Schramm, standing on the balcony of her house in the trees, c. 1930. Note the ladder at left, indicating that visitors are welcome at the moment.

Gretchen Riggs

Gretchen Riggs

GRETCHEN WAS THEATRICAL. Gretchen was grand. Gretchen was one of a kind. Gretchen fit in perfectly in Fairhope and nowhere else on the planet.

She was born in Toledo, Iowa, in 1888. Although in the same state in which the Fairhope Single Tax Corporation was created, she had nothing to do with that. She was a pianist, poet, and actress, and she had a mind of her own.

Gretchen was born into an upper-class family and reared to be a Victorian lady. She had other ideas. Her German family was strict. Her parents found her Bohemian nature and youthful rebelliousness not only shocking but unacceptable. Somehow she was able to break these bonds and get away—to Rutgers University in New Jersey, later to the University of Heidelberg, and then New York to study drama with Mme. Alberti, a drama teacher of the early days of the twentieth century. The history is dim here—a budding career as a New York actress, marriage to a doctor, life in New Jersey. Not much was written about her from that period, except for a hint that all was not well. By the time she got to Fairhope (for the first time in 1922 on a visit) she was ready to change her life.

The Chain I Wear for You

The chain, with amulet of secret wife,
Which secret love has soldered to its links,
And which you tossed about my throat and life,
Lies hidden under secret frills. Who thinks
That I, so gentle and serene, do wear
So strangely wrought an amulet as this,
Whose mold was cast in blazing passion's glare
And etched in bitter acid of your kiss?
How sad that I must always be serene,
Must never tear the frills from off my throat,
Must fool the patterned world with gracious mien,
Must choke the song which clamors for its rote!

Oh, easier far to play Love's silly game
Than be a secret wife—with wifehood's claim.

In her scrapbook I found this poem, which revealed a side of
Gretchen I would never in my wildest dreams have suspected. With its
overtones of Edna St. Vincent Millay, the sonnet clearly refers to a
forbidden love—this from our always dignified, never prepossessing
character actress rather than leading lady! Was it a personal reference?
About the situation that inspired her wonderful poem, Gretchen never
revealed a thing.

There were anecdotes she related happily. When Dr. Riggs was
directed to find a suitable Southern locale for his health, Gretchen
inquired of her friend, travel writer Helen Maupin, asking where in
the South they could possibly tolerate living, being avant-garde in
their tastes and artistic in their temperament. Maupin didn't hesitate
for a moment. Reportedly Ms. Maupin said, "Fairhope, Alabama!
There are so many freaks there they'll never even notice you."

They began visiting Fairhope at once, and both loved it, although
Dr. Riggs never lived in town for long. He probably saw it as a place for
Gretchen to thrive—alone. The family doesn't say much about that.

They had two children. Little Gail, a shy, quiet child, was so overwhelmed by her mother's strong will and personality that even Gretchen knew she was not providing the best environment for her. It was decided that it was better that Gail live with her grandparents rather than with her mother, so she did not dwell in Fairhope until her own final years.

The Gretchen Riggs I came to know was interesting and fun, even though she was strong and could be dictatorial. She taught piano, and had her house designed with a piano space so large that she could give concerts in it. She and Margaret ("Darge") Wharton used to work together on dual piano concerts—or was that "dueling piano" concerts? Both were dramatic, both were talented musicians, both probably relished the competition on the keyboard. Piney Gaston, a lifelong friend, was too casual about the piano for Gretchen's demanding taste. Piney loved to play for fun and entertainment. Gretchen, serious and Germanic about technique, would have none of this approach.

Like her own Gail, as a child I found Gretchen intimidating, but I came to know her through our mutual interest in theatre. She had brought materials for puppet making to the Organic School when I was a child, with a foul-smelling homemade papier-mâché that we molded over light bulbs, painted, and then somehow extricated the glass from inside.

As a teenager I became interested in theatre in earnest. If interested in the theatre in the 1940s or '50s, ultimately you had to deal with Gretchen Riggs. Her artistic reputation was to last her whole life. She was working with amateur groups and student groups into her nineties.

Her appearance alone was off-putting. She was tall, white-haired, imposing, with intense, bulging brown eyes, a horsey mouth, a fine large nose, and a way of speaking that commanded attention. This outward persona, I would later learn, masked a *joie de vivre*, a genuine delight in ideas, and a keen interest in other people.

All of her life young people gravitated to her, and her influence on them was profound. In her they saw the possibility of a life lived on one's own terms, right to the end. She grew old, but never lost the ability to appreciate every phase of life. She said that was there was unity in life and death, and that both could be experienced with joy.

Her acceptance of the cycles of life was a marvel to young people, who could identify with her exuberance, yet could not fathom what being old would be like. She made her own way of meeting that challenge one that interested those at the beginning of the journey.

In play production, all the players were to "give to the center"—to relinquish the self in support of the whole. The attempt was to create harmony of effort and result in a work of art.

In her later years, she organized a little meditation group with the hope that it would help her "keep from slipping to the other side."

An omnivorous reader, she became interested in the occult and owned a crystal ball, which she used on occasion, very much in private, to consult with those who had gone before. Her young colleague Owen Minnich described these sessions in great earnest many years later, claiming that he once borrowed her crystal ball and took it home. He tried to invoke its power, and suddenly in the ball he viewed a cousin of his lying dead in a distant location. Chilled by the vision, he inquired about the cousin and learned that she had indeed just died. With great trepidation he returned the object to Gretchen, who was bemused by his story.

She enjoyed a fierce rivalry with her colleague Nancy Head as they vied for control of Theatre 98, a reincarnation of Fairhope's old Little Theatre. During rehearsals of a play she was directing, Gretchen had an accident that required hospitalization. When her artist friend Mary Rapp came to commiserate with her in the hospital, Gretchen would not be appeased. "I know what really caused this," she told Mary in all ominous seriousness, bidding her to come closer to hear a confidence. "Nancy Head put a hex on me, " she told Mary in a stage whisper.

On January 16, 1981, Gretchen Riggs died. A memorial service was held for her several months later at St. James' Episcopal Church, conducted by the gentle Rev. William Hill.

Mary Rapp recalls the beautiful evening, when, as she entered the sanctuary, she noticed a young cat at the door, watching the people come in. The cat seemed to sense the solemnity of the occasion, nodding its head in a dignified way. The animal appeared to be greeting the crowd that packed the little church. It almost seemed to Mary as if the cat were counting the house.

The cat strutted quietly as the crowd gathered, observing that all had taken their places, and sat at the back of the church throughout the service in reverent silence. Rev. Hill was also aware of this feline visitor, and also noted its sense of belonging at the memorial.

Days later, Mary asked Bill Hill where that cat had come from.

"I never saw it before," said the reverend. "And, after everybody went home that evening, the cat departed too. I've never seen it again."

Craig Sheldon, 1976

Craig Sheldon

H E WAS A GROWNUP who seemed like a child. Tall, humorous, hot-tempered yet usually laughing, he was not a man a child would call "Mr. Sheldon." But to be respectful, because he was an artist and a writer, youngsters called him Craig Sheldon.

Born in 1917 in Tennessee, he lived a storybook life—complete with youthful adventures—later living in a homemade castle with a delightful, loving wife and a passel of children. Craig had a way with words, a quick wit. He wrote a weekly column for the *Fairhope Courier* for twenty years. His fertile imagination created a unique universe for him. His column, "Knee Deep in Fly Creek," recorded his conversations with an irreverent frog named Godfrey. His writing was deft, but his art was astonishing.

He created carvings of nonexistent fantasy "critters" such as the "Head-Holding High-Hopper," a bizarre grasshopper-like figure with hands atop its head; or a three-foot column adorned with human ears of many sizes and types, entitled "Listening Post."

The craftsmanship was undeniable, but the hours of work that went into the carving of one single, perfect replica of a blue crab might arguably be considered something other than art. That is, if *Art* was serious, universal, challenging, this work might be a little bit too lovable. Craig's work was accessible to all, including children and old ladies.

People said he was a genius. That's an overused word. However, now that we have seen the many levels of his work, it is hard to deny that those people were probably right about Craig Sheldon. He never turned out less than his best, and he worked tirelessly on details, creating perfection in small things, which were to him the important things. His vision was as obvious as it was profound.

He took a child's delight in nature and in fantasy, and at times the two elements overlapped for him. And to his soul, he was an artist. From a piece of wood he could create a breathtakingly lifelike creature—an insect, perhaps, or a crustacean, or a fantasy combination of real life and whimsy. The grain became the lines within a wing or the creases of a shell. The objects he carved took on an air of life, as though the wood were always intended to be this insect, that crab, this owl, or that menacing little figure wearing a robe and carrying a weapon. His human figures were often accompanied by a legend that made a political point.

He was known for his ability to create humor out of serious matters. His weekly column in the *Fairhope Courier* bore a self-created caricature of Craig sitting at his typewriter in water up to his knees, surrounded with reeds, rushes, and bullfrogs, depicting Craig literally knee-deep in Fly Creek. His writings were usually political commentary, but deliciously couched in his own combination of irony, apt description, crystalline wit, and exaggerated outrage.

Sheldon was born into a tempestuous home in a hardscrabble time. Always self-sufficient, he once ran away to escape the wrath of his alcoholic stepfather. The family moved innumerable times during his childhood. The demanding S. W. Alexander, principal of Fairhope High School, expelled the young Craig for some infraction lost to history. He had no choice but to go to the other school in town, the Organic School. This seemed a more logical choice anyway, since it taught woodworking and other things he loved to do. It was a black day for him, however, when he entered Organic and discovered that Mr. Alexander had left the public school to become the new principal *there*. He always said he didn't know who was bothered most about his matriculation at Organic, he or Mr. Alexander.

After graduation, he went off on his own to Alaska, where he claimed to have shot a bear at point-blank range, ice-skated with Mae West, and sold hooch to Bing Crosby. He developed a talent for telling stories.

Craig liked making a spectacle out of himself. Virginia Austin, a newcomer to Fairhope from Mobile in the 1950s, told her children he "just wanted to become the town character." I was a teenager when I heard this, and I couldn't understand it. In a town as full of characters as Fairhope, was there a competition? Nonsense. Craig was always Craig, and couldn't have been more of a character if he actually tried.

He liked wearing hats, swinging canes, and swaggering through town. He liked to argue. He liked to laugh. He liked to shock, but he never did anything just for shock value. He was an original.

We took Craig Sheldon for granted then. He was as likely as not to write obscenities in the Guest Book at the Eastern Shore Art Center, to take a grandchild off for a forbidden ice cream sundae, or to mount his own campaign against Fidel Castro by participating in Alpha 66, a guerrilla maritime mission to reclaim Cuba.

His irascibility was countered by his charm. And underlying it all was his vision, his art, and his intemperate devotion to his own instincts. A consummate craftsman and a driven artist, he did not live a tidy life. But his legacy will always be part of Fairhope—including the home he lived in—a handmade castle he built out of local clay tiles, old drink bottles, shells, and found objects. This place of residence inspired his daughter Pagan and her husband, artist Dean Mosher, to build a similar one right next door for their family. The two unorthodox "castles" make a statement for all to see.

There will probably always be memories, quotations, and tall tales up and down the Eastern Shore about the man. But it is through his work that we best recall the paradox—intelligence, sensitivity, art, rage, and tenderness—all playing hide and seek behind a comic mask.

Anna Braune

Anna Braune

BOB BELL DESCRIBES his first encounter with the impressive Anna Braune, Fairhope's librarian of the 1950s, who also happened to be a published author and illustrator of children's books:

...My brothers and I spent a lot of time on the waterfront, and one day we were diving off the Big Pier when suddenly this dignified young woman appeared with a white-haired older woman. The young woman yelled to us that it was dangerous to be diving from the pier. We thanked her and kept right on, since the early-morning tide made the water quite deep. I knew who she was.

I wanted to meet her, of course, since she was a writer and writers fascinated me. Later on, Barbara Key, the Fairhope High School teacher who had directed me in a play, took me around and introduced me, and Anna and I became instant friends.

I always admired her work and her wonderful perception of the world. She used to show me her drawings and pastels, and I saw the still unpublished plates from *The Bojabi Tree*. Her inscribed copy to me said, "To Bobby Bell, who was born to have cream on his bojabi." I used to love to look at her drawing of an elegant shrimp at Spanish Fort. She used to talk about the creatures she had drawn or painted. I remember especially the little mouse being courted by a bullfrog, and she pointed out that Miss Mouse was showing emotion only at the very tip of her tail.

She was immensely talented, and I am glad to have the little drawing of two children, which hangs in a spot on my upper stair which I can see from where I am now sitting, and the charcoal of me that I simply do not remember her doing. Just this year I read, for the first time, *Honey Chile*. I don't know why I never did before. I was again impressed with her wonderful feeling about people, black and white. Some might call this idyllic little story a naïve view of life in the South, but these would be people who did not know her. Anna's only prejudices were reserved for bigots and hatemongers. In her quiet way she embraced everyone else. She was one of the dozen or so people who made a great difference in my life.

Miss Braune made a difference in many lives. There were children who practically lived at the library, reading all the books on the shelves, exploring the museum room with its local rocks, arrowheads, examples of taxidermy of the local fauna, and other natural history artifacts. Anna Braune knew all about books and writers and had a friendly, easy way with children. She would later reflect, "I always liked bad children. I found them congenial."

Anna had begun life as an artist, drawing pictures at the age of three. Her father, Gustave Braune, was a university professor. Born in Albany, New York, she lived in Cincinnati, Ohio, until her father was made the dean of the School of Engineering at the University of North Carolina at Chapel Hill.

Her art took her to the Cincinnati School of Design and the New York School of Art and Design. For two years she lived in Connecticut and commuted to New York City, where Lord & Taylor commissioned her and another artist to design movable murals as an innovative interior design concept. These were large screens of linen and silk, with dramatic figures like leopards and florals painted on them. The idea was that apartment dwellers and renters of houses could take their "walls" with them when they moved. Anna's panels were primarily designed for children's rooms, and her mural of rabbits dashing around a maypole was selected for the Paris Exhibition.

Although a very modest, soft-spoken young lady, Anna loved the excitement of New York. She always professed shyness, and claimed to have been "shaking like a leaf" when presenting her drawings in the offices of prestigious publishers like Random House and Doubleday. Yet she did it, often, and the drawings sold. The art spoke for her.

She left the New York School of Art and Design on her own, finding it "too commercial." She won a fellowship to study at Menton in France, and unfortunately had to leave after only two weeks when her father died suddenly. She moved back to the States to stay with her mother. The two divided their time between Chapel Hill and Fairhope from then on.

Anna painted with a blend of precision and whimsy. Her drawings are distinctly hers, whether of children holding hands or a jumbo shrimp dressed up in formal attire. Animals with human characteristics were a specialty. Once when asked how she had been able to create so realistic a fox, she replied, "I was that fox the whole time I was painting him." This personalization of her work may shed light on her comment to Bob Bell about the mouse's reaction to the bullfrog.

In the 1930s she was to create her most celebrated work, the lovely children's book *Honey Chile*. As Bob noted earlier, *Honey Chile* is not easy to take today, unless you knew Miss Braune and her devotion to her subjects. It tells the story of a little girl who summers in the South and is tended to by an understanding black "Mammy," who is also the mother of the children with whom she plays. The book is full of old-fashioned Negro dialect, considered charming in the 1930s, and certainly portrayed with accuracy and affection by the author. It may take time before we can comfortably revisit this work.

It also may be difficult to conceive of how successful it was. *Honey Chile* was greeted with rave reviews in the press, north and south. It was a best-selling children's book. Marietta Johnson sent a note to

Eleanor Roosevelt recommending it, and taking it upon herself to express Fairhope's pride in the accomplishments of the young writer/illustrator.

Her ephemeral nature and delicate style make Anna Braune a difficult subject to write about, because in memory she seems almost otherworldly. Yet Anna Braune was very much of this world. She was politically engaged and even *avant-garde*. She was an interesting paradox of gentle/unassuming with sophisticated/sharp. And, as the children who surrounded her would be quick to state today, she was revered and enjoyed too.

In the scrapbook she kept at the end of her life, there is a Christmas card she received from Bob Bell in 1986. She was living in a nursing home at that time, as she battled crippling diseases including myasthenia gravis and multiple sclerosis.

Bob's letter seemed to be reaching into the very heart of their long, loving relationship, to speak almost in her own voice.

Dearest Anna—

I remember Christmases past when I was home from school and we would sit in front of your fire and catch up on things. The world has since suffered without us to solve its problems in such a thoughtful and civilized way. But we left a legacy. Do you wonder if books talk to each other after librarians turn out the lights and go home? You and I were smart enough to have names beginning with B, so our novels sit side by side in the Fairhope Public Library, and I suspect they have done some talking. I just hope that someone named Besterman or Blackford doesn't come along and separate us. Wouldn't that be a shame?

I do so love all our days, and I love you. Let's think something splendid about each other on Christmas Day. O.K.?

Love,
Bobby

Afterword

A "BUTTERFLY" TREE OR BUSH is a horticultural phenomenon. Certain species of plant attract butterflies, which alight upon them, sometimes all at once, creating a visual spectacle that is very pleasing to the human spirit.

Fairhope itself is a butterfly tree. Its practical roots of political reform plunge deep below the surface of the ground, not visible to the casual observer, but necessary to the existence of the tree. Like a fragrant, red-blossomed shrub, it confronts each new season with changes that subtly seduce the susceptible. It reaches out to a natural network, beckoning its own in an almost biological way. Itinerant species move here to live out their brief lifetimes.

At one time those who moved to Fairhope did so out of a commitment to a life of the mind. It is stretching the metaphor beyond the breaking point to call these people "butterflies," unless we redefine the term to mean people with a beauty made even more beautiful in combination with that of others.

What this book has done is introduce you to some aspects of Fairhope's past, through stories of its places, characters, and situations that happened within my memory. Through its pages you have started your own journey toward discovering the village as it once was.

119

Today we see the dichotomy of old and new, and with it comes an exciting opportunity. The city is prettier and more prosperous. It is impossible to predict how things will go, but there is an air of optimism and niceness in the air.

There is no question that today we yearn for something undefined. In Fairhope that yearning is palpable. Perhaps the dreams of the early settlers are affecting us in ways we don't acknowledge. In some instances they conformed to the outside world; in some they did not. They had the blessing of a town in which either choice was acceptable. The comfort of this place enabled them to do good works and influence coming generations simply by being themselves.

This is possible for each of us. We still have our parks, laid out a century ago. We have Fairhope's legacy of dreams for a better world. We have the land the early Single-Taxers saved for us. And we have our own hopes for better things for coming generations. The promise of Fairhope's founders is the promise we share in our own lives here. We know the potential and the magic of the place itself.

And somewhere in a gully on a particular day in a certain season, the fortunate wanderer will actually find a tree covered in butterflies. Stay for a moment if you can. It should not be a surprise, even if it is not expected, if a shadow dances among the leaves, a face appears (or seems to), even a community of phantoms from the past. Here you will find answers, questions, and a host of stories.